100+ IDEAS FOR DRAMA

100 + Ideas for Drama

Anna Scher
and
Charles Verrall

HEINEMANN EDUCATIONAL BOOKS
LONDON

Heinemann Educational Books Ltd
22 Bedford Square, London WC1B 3HH

LONDON EDINBURGH MELBOURNE AUCKLAND
SINGAPORE KUALA LUMPUR NEW DELHI
IBADAN NAIROBI JOHANNESBURG
PORTSMOUTH (NH) KINGSTON

ISBN 0 435 18799 6

Printed in Great Britain by
Richard Clay Ltd, Bungay, Suffolk

Contents

The photograph on the front cover is reproduced by courtesy of Derek Turner. The photographs on the back cover are reproduced by courtesy of Nova Munda Photography.

Introduction

WHY WE ARE WRITING THIS BOOK

We have been running the Anna Scher Children's Theatre since 1968, and in that time we have developed and used literally hundreds of different ideas in drama. We receive a large number of visitors from all parts of the world, as well as running Drama Workshop Courses for students, teachers, social workers, etc., and we are also sent hundreds of letters asking for advice and help. One of the things that all these people want is to build up a fund of practical ideas which they can use, be they a teacher faced with a new class, a social worker starting a neighbourhood drama group, or a student working in an improvisation group.

The aim of the book is to fill this need.

WHAT THIS BOOK IS

It is a recipe book containing hundreds of drama ideas. It is not our intention that the recipes should be followed slavishly; we hope that the book will be used as a source book in which material can be found which can be adapted and developed for use in any particular situation. To this end we have as far as possible presented ideas open-endedly, suggesting as many developments and variations as possible, so that each reader can use the ideas in his or her own way.

Again, in this book we do not lay down a suggested course or syllabus in drama; we hope that our ideas could be usefully incorporated in any teaching programme. Some of the ideas are of our own devising, others are old and well known; all of them have been tried and tested and found to work with a wide range of children and adults.

1

WHO THIS BOOK IS FOR

Teachers, students at Colleges of Education (not just those specializing in drama for secondary schools but also all those who will be working in primary schools, where most teachers take some drama); social workers; playgroup leaders; librarians; people involved in community projects; parents looking for things for their children, and their children's friends, to do in the holidays; students at drama schools and university drama courses; actors; fringe, underground and student theatre groups; and everyone interested in children's theatre or theatre generally.

We are not just thinking of drama taking place in schools: although we have generally used the words 'class' and 'teacher', the descriptions could equally well apply to other situations. So for 'class' you can read 'drama group', 'club', 'cub pack', 'adventure playground', 'amateur dramatic society' and so on. Likewise, we have generally used the word 'children' but many of the ideas can be just as successfully used with adults.

HOW THE BOOK IS LAID OUT

We have divided the book up into chapters, each chapter containing ideas of a particular type: 'Games', 'The Spoken Word', 'Warm-Ups, Mime and Movement', 'Character, Props and Costumes', 'Situation Drama and Improvised Plays', and 'Technique'. These are, of course, not watertight divisions, merely convenient ones. The contents of the chapters overlap a great deal, and it was in some cases difficult to decide which chapter a particular idea should go into.

We have not split up the chapters into age ranges, 'Drama for Juniors' or 'Drama for Teenagers', for example, because children vary so much that one cannot

lay down any hard and fast rules. While there are
obviously some ideas that are for adults and near adults
only, and others for infants only, a great deal depends on
the child's age, ability and stage of development, and
also on what experience they have had of drama. Some
groups of children simply have more grown-up tastes
than others. Many ideas can be used at a variety of
different age-levels, by altering the presentation in a way
appropriate to the age group you are working with.

In any class or other drama group there will be individuals working at different stages at the same time (e.g.
some children will be ready to do character work long
before others). This is no disadvantage. In our own
experience, we typically work with groups with age
range six to eleven, or eleven to eighteen — with some
children attending for the first time working in the same
group as others with several years experience of drama.
A spread of age, ability and experience in a group can be
an advantage rather than a handicap. Children learn from
each other.

Usually we don't mention the purpose of individual
exercises — in some cases the purpose is obvious — but in
other cases different teachers and classes will use the
ideas in varying ways and derive different benefits from
them. Our main aim in this book is to provide tools that
can be used, rather than to theorize on the structure that
can be built with them.

WHAT DO CHILDREN GAIN FROM DRAMA?

First and above all — enjoyment. Then comes a wide
range of other benefits: it provides an outlet for self-
expression and helps the development of imagination and
artistic awareness; it increases social awareness
(particularly through role play), mental awareness,
fluency of speech, self-knowledge, self-respect, self-

discipline and self-confidence. It gives children the opportunity to learn how to co-operate with others and helps develop orderly thinking and the ability to organize. It improves physical co-ordination and physical fitness. It may also have a therapeutic effect, through helping children to deal with their real life problems, or a cathartic effect, by enabling them to act out violence and frustration. It provides social and moral training, and helps young people to mature emotionally, preparing them for adult life.

Drama is a marvellous vehicle for general knowledge, and in schools there are many ways in which it can be linked with English, History, Art, Music, etc. It also provides a good outlet for the ability of bright but non-academically-minded children, and also gives opportunities to do well for children on whom society may tend to force low expectations, for racial or other reasons.

The benefits do not only accrue through children participating actively in drama; they can also learn from observing others, particularly if they are encouraged to watch positively and critically by being asked to comment and give praise afterwards.

PLAY, DRAMA AND THEATRE

Play, Drama and Theatre are linked, and each is a development of the other. There is a great deal to be gained by children at each level. Each is valuable for its own sake, but Play leads to Drama, and Drama leads to Theatre.

At the 'Drama' stage, thoughts and feelings are experienced and shared by members of a participating group. In time we learn to communicate these to others, so that at the 'Theatre' stage, because of the use of technique, people not involved in the action — a whole roomful of people — can share in the experience too.

DISCIPLINE

One of the questions we are most frequently asked is how do we maintain order, especially when taking large classes of eighty-plus, as we often do. We believe in *organized* drama — the first thing the children learn is to be a *good audience* — a disciplined framework gives children freedom to express themselves in a satisfying way.

Here are ten discipline 'tips' which we hope will be useful to student-teachers:

1 *Holding interest.* In order to hold a child's interest the lesson must be well prepared and interesting for the child. Try and look at it from the child's point of view, as well as your own.

2 *Mutual respect.* When you talk they listen to you, when they talk you listen to them — the whole class listens to them — it works both ways.

3 *Self confidence.* Usually, you're bigger than they are — who would challenge a giant? If you're not bigger than them, think of the zoo-keeper entering a cage with a lion in it. He behaves calmly and confidently — and the lion immediately co-operates. So don't think yourself into a weak position before you even start. Put yourself into a positive frame of mind. Have everything prepared and ready — then you can look forward to each lesson. Get them to sit down while you're standing — this gives you a strong psychological advantage. Start off firmly — after a while it is easy to relax a little — but it is very difficult to do the reverse, if you have been starting off too casually.

4 The word *'Freeze'* uttered crisply is valuable in drama, likewise *'Stop'* rather than 'stop talking'. 'Freeze' can be

used in a play context. 'When I say "freeze" everyone must stop absolutely still like a statue: it's as if I'd gone into a roomful of Madam Tussaud's waxworks. You mustn't move a muscle! Freeze!' It works.

5 The *tone* of your voice — low key is very effective. Constant shouting is *not*. Say a few words loudly to get people's attention and then gradually drop your voice to a pleasant, quiet, conversational level. The children will get used to you talking in a constantly quiet voice and having established this as the norm there will be little or no need to raise your voice.

6 Gimmicks like 'hands on heads', 'look at my finger', the drawing pin 'test' are useful with younger children if used occasionally. The drawing pin 'test' cannot really be carried out with any group more than once a term. Raise your hand high, holding in it one small brass drawing pin. 'Now we cannot begin until we have done the drawing pin "test". I want absolute quiet in this room; so quiet that when I drop the drawing pin I want to hear it as clear as can be.' Wait for quiet — and drop the pin!

7 Taking away a break is quite an effective sanction.

8 The teacher's *appearance* is important. The children care how you look and they react to the way you look.

9 Giving special *attention* to the difficult child often cures the difficulty. Give a dog a bad name — it's a very unfortunate child that is labelled all the way up the school. Boys and girls know when they have a bad name. Knowing the children really well as individuals and having continuous relationships with them is very important.

10 Concentration exercise. First define the meaning of the word *concentration* — 'keeping your mind on some-

thing'; to do a job well you must concentrate — *'If a job is worth doing it's worth doing well'*. Simple concentration exercises like closing the eyes and listening to the teacher's voice can have a very soothing effect.

The more *energy,* mental and physical, you can put into your work the more effective you will be, and you will get a better response from the children. If you are physically fit you are less likely to get tired and bad-tempered at the end of a long day.

Encouragement and rewards are much more effective than punishments, as well as being kinder; at the same time, when the need arises one must not be afraid to say 'No', decisively and firmly.

DRAMA IN DIFFICULT SITUATIONS

Many of you are, or soon will be, attempting to teach drama in tough schools or other difficult situations, particularly in educational priority areas in the big cities.

By a 'tough' school we mean one with high staff turnover, few experienced teachers, little contact between parents and staff, poor discipline, little encouragement given to the children at home, high rates of truancy and delinquency, bad housing conditions, and all the rest of it. Many of the children will view school as an unpleasant institution which they dislike having to attend. By the age of fourteen or fifteen, they are likely to be hostile, uncooperative or apathetic towards drama.

What is one to do in a first lesson with such a group?

To start with, you can only hope for fairly limited success. You are being asked to fight battles that may have been lost years before. If drama is a compulsory subject no teacher should feel they have failed if the customers don't like it — why should young adults enjoy doing what they are forced to do against their will, however much it is supposed to be for their own good? They think of themselves as being entirely grown up, even if they aren't, and they don't like being treated or referred to as 'children' or 'kids'.

One way of beginning with a new class is through discussion, or Speakeasy, choosing a subject which they are likely to have a strong interest in. This bypasses any inhibitions they may have about actually getting up and doing things. You will need to be a strong chairman, keeping the discussion to the point and insisting on only one person speaking at a time; they will accept this necessary discipline as fair, as each of them will want the others to listen while they have their own say. While the discussion is going on you will be able to observe the boys and girls and get to know them, and they will be getting to know you.

Another way of starting off is through games, choosing those which are appropriate to the age group you are working with. Through games they will become used to getting on their feet and moving around, without being called upon to do anything the least bit arty or unmanly. Also, they will accept the discipline that is necessary for playing a game, again on the grounds of fairness. Possible games are Dog and Bone, The Hunter and the Hunted, and Statues, which introduces the vital work 'Freeze'.

Then you can start on simple improvised situation drama using a simple format (not too many people), themes close to everyday life, and situations about which they will feel strongly, e.g.

a girl comes home two hours late from the disco and finds her Mum waiting for her;
a boy must tell his friend that he has taken his

fashionable new jacket and lost it;
two girls find out by accident that they have been
going out with the same boy, leading to a jealous
argument.

You can give plenty of praise and encouragement,
while at the same time showing that you will be looking
for a high standard of work. (In a single sex school your
choice of situations will be restricted: one way round it
is to work with a neighbouring school of opposite sex,
if this can be arranged.)

Another important point is to apply a little group
psychology. In most classes there is one person with an
extroverted, dominant personality, a natural group
leader; you can spot him straightaway. Give him plenty
of attention and get him on your side; his attitude will
influence the others.

After this you must play it by ear. Don't let them get
bored. Be ready to change your plan. If you try an idea
and it doesn't work, drop it and try something else. If
in a first lesson you try ten ideas and only one of them
works, then count that as a success because now you
will have something to build on next time. Gradually
they will accept you, and even begin to enjoy themselves.

CHILDREN'S DEVELOPMENT IN DRAMA

If the first prerequisite for good drama is order, then
one of the first things that children must learn in drama
is to be a good audience. The division into performers
and audience is temporary; everyone spends some of
their time in each, and the audience is encouraged to
listen and watch intelligently. The children will learn from
each other, in the same way as they like to hear each
other's compositions in English, sharing ideas and helping
one another.

Two ways in which a child's development in drama can be hindered are:

1 By the teacher asking too little: children's work improves fastest when their teachers have high expectations of them. Far more children are potentially talented than is generally recognized — their ability just has to be discovered and encouraged at the right time. So a good working principle is to assume that *every* child has talent waiting to be found and encouraged.
2 By the teacher asking too much: there is no surer way of damaging a child's confidence than by asking him to do something which is too difficult or which he is not yet ready for. Young children, particularly, are not themselves the best judges of what they can handle.

So one should always be asking for a little bit more from a child, but not too much more, eventually stretching them fully; they will respond to being stretched — but never force them.

Clearly, in order to be able to judge what you should be asking of each individual child, you must observe them closely. What are they doing in the lesson? How are they reacting? Which one needs encouraging? Which has reached an important jumping-off point and is ready to move on?

Treat them as individuals; they are all different. Individual work is valuable for their personal development. Too many children are only treated as part of a crowd all their lives.

Keep up to date with the children's interests and fashions. This way you will understand the same language; you can do this without pretending to be one of them.

If you are working in a school get to know the boys and girls outside the school situation; this will help to build their confidence and trust in you, which takes time.

If you take them out, keep an Outings Book and make sure that everyone gets their turn, so that it is fair, and seen to be fair.

EDUCATIONAL DRAMA AND PERFORMANCE DRAMA

A dogma has grown up that the presence of any element of performance in drama is incompatible with educational value, and that the teaching of dramatic technique will stifle children's creativity. In our opinion, this view is mistaken.

In the past 'The School Play' was often produced by a teacher with no drama training and with children with no drama experience. In this situation the difficulties of getting children to learn their lines, deliver them audibly and remember their moves would force creative self-expression to take a back seat. However, this is not the result of attempting performance drama, it is the result of attempting performance drama without proper preparation.

The point is that the educational benefit of drama is not just limited to the exploration and expression of the child's own feelings and ideas by itself. No man is an island, and sooner or later the child needs to communicate those feelings and ideas with other people, and to receive similar communication from them. The more effectively this can be done, the more satisfactory the experience will be, and this is where the teaching of drama technique comes in: it is taught so that the children's desire to communicate will not be frustrated by their lack of the best means with which to do so.

So, points of technique can be introduced in a positive way, as the need arises in the children's own work, starting with simple ones such as: 'If you want people to hear you, you've got to speak loudly enough for them to do so', or 'If you start giggling in the middle of a piece of drama, it means you've stopped believing in what you're doing, and so will everybody else'. Technique in drama is not an end in itself, just the means to an end, as it is in any art, craft or skill, be it music, pottery or football.

There are so many conflicting theories of how drama should be taught — whether the teacher should take an active role, whether it should be 'child-centred' and so on — how is the individual teacher to choose between them? The only answer is to study them all and develop your own synthesis, not automatically adopting whatever is fashionable, or whatever is traditional, but by reading round the subject, and observing and absorbing other people's methods, to find out what best suits you and the children you are working with.

BELIEVABILITY

However much fantasy you use in drama, never lose touch with reality. The real world is not populated with woodcutters and swordfighters, so don't spend too much time in drama on chopping wood and fighting with swords.

To establish a base of realism right from the start, you must have situations which are real to the children — which they can identify with and believe in. Believability in any given situation is essential.

HIGH STANDARDS

It is important not to confuse an emphasis on a high standard of work with the fostering of an over-competitive attitude. There is a welcome tendency in education to favour co-operation rather than competition, but this should not lead to a decline in standards.

Children want to learn to do drama properly, just as they want to do proper experiments in science.

THE STRUCTURE OF A LESSON

Everyone will want to devise their own style and methods, but to give an idea of the pattern in which the ideas in this book have been developed: in a typical session of one and a half hours, we would plan to use about fifteen items, of which about 40 per cent would have the entire class working together, 40 per cent would be in groups of two or more, and 20 per cent would have children working individually. This is approximately the same for all age groups, with slightly more class and group work with younger children and slightly less with older ones. Music is used for about 30 per cent of items.

Have your lesson prepared well in advance. Make sure that the record player and other equipment is working properly, that the records are ready in correct order, and that anything else you will need is on hand. The person in charge of the session must not rely on anyone else to do this, he must do it himself.

Although your lesson will have been prepared, you must be ready to sense the changing mood of the class and vary your programme accordingly — skipping a couple of items, changing the tempo, staying with something that is getting interesting and developing it.

To hold the interest of the class you will need to keep the pace of the lesson going well and to maintain continuity — no long gaps while the room is being rearranged or you decide what to do next.

Staying with a single topic for a long time does not necessarily enable you to explore it any more deeply. Speed need not lead to superficiality — it makes it possible to obtain a more intense degree of concentration, which could not be maintained for a longer period of time.

Remember that you cannot expect improvisation to
come out of thin air. People must have a framework to
work within. When working on an improvisation idea
for the first ime, you will need to give a fair amount of
guidance and make plenty of suggestions. Then, with
experience, the children will learn how to draw on their
imagination and can gradually be given a more open
brief.

STARTING A DRAMA CLUB

One of the ways to build up drama in a school is to
invite children to join a drama club which they attend of
their own volition. It is entirely optional, they will come
because they want to come. This puts the teacher in a
strong position. The interest is there, it is now up to you
to sustain that interest.

So to begin with, just announce at School Assembly,
or in your classes, that you are going to start a drama
club in the lunch-hour and/or after school, and that all
those interested will be most welcome to attend. You
might add as a foretaste the kind of activities you will
be doing — there'll be music and movement, games,
mask work, plays — whet their appetites from the word
go.

If you do not work in a school and want to start an
independent drama club you will need to find suitable
premises: a church hall or community hall that can be
hired. Alternatively, you can work within an already
existing organization such as a youth club. Posters
(clearly stating time and place) can be displayed in
adventure playgrounds, youth clubs or schools (with
the Head's permission). Children don't always read
posters so it is most important that you yourself are the
advertisement for the drama club; if you start with a
small nucleus of boys and girls you already know, word

will soon spread among both parents and children and numbers will grow.

If you are not under the aegis of any official body you will have to make sure the premises you are using are considered suitable by the local authority, and you will also need to insure against injury that may be suffered by any child in your care.

Equipment

The following is a list of simple equipment which will be most useful for the drama club:

Basic equipment

Record player and records	Box of Hats
Costumes	Scarves
Stage blocks	Masks
Table, chairs	Wigs
Mirror	Bags
Notice board	

Props

Telephone	Pack of cards
Bell	Tea things — Tea-pot
Vase of flowers (plastic)	and mugs
Newspaper	Tray
Doll in shawl	Guns
Football rattle	Clock
Rubber gloves	Chalk
Knitting	Bus stop
Books	Pairs of glasses
	Iron

Most of these props will probably be brought in by the children themselves. Get some large cardboard boxes and cover them in attractive coloured paper, labelling

them 'Hats', 'Scarves', 'Masks', 'Wigs', 'Bags'. If you ask
the children to search round for old hats, etc. at home,
you will soon be inundated with them. Old mirrors,
masks, and all kinds of other oddments can be found in
street markets. If you have someone who is skilled at
carpentry they can make a bus-stop, and also a bench,
which is very useful. A television set, with the inside
taken out to make it lighter, is useful for every home
scene, but you can use a stage block to represent this
equally well. A large tray is useful to hold your small
props like the iron, knitting, vase of flowers, etc., and is
convenient if you have to store everything away at the
end of a session. A dress rail obtained from a shopfitters
is invaluable for your costumes; better than a dressing-up
box where the clothes can't all be seen at once and also
tend to get crumpled. Costumes such as roomy dressing
gowns, raincoats, housecoats, cloaks, nightgowns,
baggy trousers and the like are much more adaptable
than pretty summer dresses and tight fitting blouses and
skirts. There will be plenty of applicants for Wardrobe
Mistress! Also have someone in charge of props. It is
important to stress from the beginning that the children
should respect the equipment and put it back in its place
after use.

RECORDS

Music can be used in a drama lesson to provide rhythm
for movement work, to set a mood, and as an aid to
concentration. The use of live music and records of
orchestral music in these ways is generally accepted; pop
records are often neglected because they are not
considered 'cultural'.

　　In our own work we use a large library of pop records,
mainly instrumental, as well as other types of music.
There is a great wealth and variety of material available,

and the use of pop music, particularly at first, enables
you to avoid the resistance you may find children have
to working with forms of music with which they are less
familiar.

There is no need to buy records. It is easy to build up
a collection by getting the children to bring in any old
pop records they no longer want; you can keep the ones
that sound useful, and give away the rest, or else sell
them in aid of a drama fund or a charity.

Second-hand and ex-jukebox records are often for
sale very cheaply on street market stalls, in junk shops,
newsagents, etc. Many budget-priced labels produce LP's
of television and film themes: the advantage of these is
that you get plenty of different moods and rhythms on
one record. Film soundtrack LP's are often good, too, for
the same reason.

Artists to look out for on old 45's are: Duane Eddy,
Sandy Nelson, Kenny Ball, B. Bumble and the Stingers,
the John Barry 7, Whistling Jack Smith, Herb Alpert,
Isaac Hayes, Junior Walker, and of course any 'Band'
or 'Orchestra'. West Indian records are often very
suitable, as well.

Whenever a new instrumental or other suitable record
gets into the charts you can buy it, thus ensuring you
have some up-to-date sounds on hand!

ONE

Games

Here are some games that are linked with drama, chosen to benefit children through improved co-ordination, agility, experience of teamwork, self-reliance, improved fluency, and general knowledge.

Games like these can provide a light-hearted way in to drama for a new class, and they can also make a good way of relaxing and letting off steam at the end of a session.

1 PHYSICAL GAMES

Up Down Freeze Game

The boys and girls all run round the room in the same direction until the teacher calls 'Freeze', when they all stop absolutely still like statues. The object of the game is to keep as still as possible. Anyone who moves is out and goes back to his place. On 'Go' the class run round the room again until the teacher calls 'Up' and everyone stops still and puts their hands in the air. Again, anyone who moves is out. And so the game continues. If the teacher calls 'Down' everyone drops to the ground; 'Heads' means hands on heads; 'Shoulders'—hands on shoulders; 'Turn'—everyone turns and stands still (which means that on 'Go' they will now run round in the opposite direction); 'One Leg'— everyone has to stand still with one foot in mid air.

As the game progresses the judging has to get more and more stringent. Anyone moving the least fraction is out (though they are allowed to blink and breathe!). They are also out if they follow the wrong instruction, stop

running, run in the wrong direction, react too slowly,
talk, or laugh. Last survivor wins the gold medal!

Who is Missing?
This is a good observation game for younger children.
They all run round the room several times. On 'Freeze —
eyes closed', they stop still and close their eyes. Then they
they are instructed to make themselves into a small ball
on the ground, their eyes closed all the time. The teacher
tiptoes towards one child and taps him on the back,
motioning him to hide outside the door. The children, who
still have their eyes closed, are told to stand: then they
are told to run round again and can, of course, open their
eyes. At 'Freeze' the teacher asks 'Who is missing?' And
so the game continues.

Pip, Squeak and Wilfred
The children stand in a circle and are given the names
Pip, Squeak, Wilfred, Pip, Squeak, Wilfred. . . . The
teacher calls out 'Pip' and all the Pips run anti-clockwise
round the outside of the circle and keep running round
until the teacher blows the whistle which means 'Home'.
On the whistle they must run round the circle to their
places *without changing direction* — even if they're only
just past their home position. The last person 'home' is
out and sits cross-legged on the ground in his place, so
that no one will trip over him. Anyone running in the
wrong direction is out as well.

While the children are running round and round, the
teacher can call 'Turn', whereupon everybody must turn
and start running in the new direction. The teacher can
repeat this several times before blowing the whistle.

When the numbers have thinned down a bit, the teacher
can call 'Pip and Squeak together' or 'Pip and Wilfred
together' or even, 'Pip, Squeak and Wilfred'. The last
person left in is the winner.

The Mad Relay

The principle is the same as in an ordinary shuttle relay when each member of a team has to run from behind the starting line to the other end of the room and back again, passing on a baton to the next person. The difference in the Mad Relay is that instead of ordinary running, more unusual forms of locomotion must be used.

Various numbers can take part. Suppose there are two teams each having four children: the number ones hold one foot in their hands and hop on the other foot to the end of the room and back. As soon as number one returns, number two sets out, running backwards. When he gets back numbers three and four together form a wheelbarrow, one walking on his hands while his legs are carried by the other. Back to number one again who this time must be carried by number two.Then number three goes backwards, jumping in the air, clapping his hands above his head and hooting at the top of his voice, and finally number four does an ordinary run.

Two umpires, one for each team, can be selected to detect unfair play; they each wear a hat and if there is any cheating that team's umpire waves his hat in the air, and with no argument, the contestant concerned has to start out from 'home' all over again.

On completion, the winning team is the first to sit at the home base, cross-legged, in silence and with hands on heads.

Any number of variations on this can be invented: running on all fours, on your knees, on your bottom – anything you like.

Cat and Mouse

Say there are thirty in the class. Divide them into four groups of seven. Each group stands in a line, stretching both arms out with fingers touching to form a wall, so that you have four parallel lines of seven making four separate walls with alleyways between them. On 'Turn' from the teacher, everyone turns a quarter-turn in the same direction to make seven lines of four people, fingertip to fingertip, with a new set of alleyways in between.

The two remaining children that are not making up the walls are chosen to be the cat and the mouse. This is a game of chase and the object is for the cat to catch the mouse. The cat chases the mouse along the alleyways but to thwart his designs the teacher frequently calls 'Turn' whereupon everyone does a quarter-turn to form the other set of walls. Neither cat nor mouse is allowed to break through the walls but must go along the alleyways. As soon as the mouse is caught, the cat and mouse change places with two children from the walls who become the new cat and mouse. This is very popular, even with older children.

Dog and Bone

There are two teams with up to twelve players each. Both teams are numbered so that the two number ones are opponents, so are the number twos, threes, fours, etc.

The teams stand behind chalk lines about twenty feet apart and the 'bone' (in the shape of a durable hat) is placed in the middle, in a position indicated by a chalked circle.

The teacher calls 'Number one' and both number ones go for the 'bone'. If team A's number one can grab the 'bone' and carry it 'home' without team B's number one touching him, team A scores a point. If team B's number one touches him before he reaches home, then team B scores the point. However, if B's number one touches the other *before* he has picked up the 'bone', then team A takes the point. The game continues with the numbers being called in any order.

The game is best played at an attacking pace so if it becomes too defensive the teacher can do a countdown from ten to zero and if no attacking move has been made before 'zero' both opponents go back to their places and there is no score for that round.

After each round the hat must be put back in the circle immediately, ready for the next number to be called. Suitable for all ages.

Pass the Shoe

The children sit in a circle. As soon as the music starts a shoe is passed round from child to child — anyone who throws it is out. Suddenly the music stops and the child who has the shoe in his hand is out. The circle gets smaller as the children are eliminated. The last child not caught holding the shoe wins. Suitable for juniors.

O'Grady Says

Everyone finds a space and stands facing the teacher. The teacher calls out 'O'Grady says do this' and performs an action (raising hands above head, clapping, putting hands on shoulders, hands on hips, marching on the spot, etc.). 'O'Grady says do this', and the teacher does a new action which everyone copies. The object of the game is for everybody to follow the action immediately if O'Grady has said to do it, but if it's just 'Do this' and not 'O'Grady says do this', they must take no notice.

The game proceeds in a fast-moving way and quick thinking on the part of the class is essential. If an action is committed without O'Grady commanding it or if anyone fails to keep up with the game, then they are out. Last man in is the winner.

Musical Bumps, Musical Chairs and Statues

Musical Bumps. Play a popular record. Everyone finds a space and dances. When the music stops everyone goes down on the ground — last one down is out. The teacher stops the music at irregular intervals and the last person left in is the winner.

Statues works in a similar way only this time when the music stops everyone stops absolutely still like statues; anyone who moves is out. The judging becomes stricter as the game proceeds. Last one in is the winner.

Musical Chairs. Start with one less chair than the number of people playing. The chairs are placed together in two lines, back to back. When the music starts the children walk round the chairs: as soon as the music stops everyone sits on a chair except one. The one who doesn't manage to get a chair is out. One chair is taken away, the music starts up again and the game continues. Last man in is the winner.

A variation of this, particularly for older boys and girls, is to play the game in twos. The partners go round the chairs hand in hand and, when the music stops, sit on a chair with one sitting on the other's knee. This is great fun, especially with a mixed class at the end of term!

The Feeling Game

This game can be linked with the five senses. You can make a reference to Helen Keller, the blind and deaf American girl having to 'see' with her fingers. One person is blindfolded and turned round several times so that he loses his bearings in the room. He is then guided on a winding path up to someone and the object of the game is for him to recognize that person by using his sense of touch. Feel the size of the person, feel the hair, the shape

of the head, the features, clothes — are they wearing a
watch or any recognizable jewellery, etc? Who is it?

The Hunter and the Hunted

One person is nominated to be the hunter, another is
the hunted. The hunter goes to one end of the room or
hall and the hunted to the opposite end. Both shut their
eyes. The object of this game is for the hunter to catch
the hunted before he can reach 'home' at the other end
of the room, but they must both keep their eyes closed —
so the only way for the hunter to 'capture' the hunted is
by *listening* for his footsteps; therefore everyone in the
room must be absolutely quiet. This is a very popular
game with all ages; we have even played it with old age
pensioners.

Adam and Eve

Everyone forms a circle and sits on the ground, making
sure there are no gaps. Adam is chosen and blindfolded.
Eve is chosen but not blindfolded. Adam and Eve must
stay within the circle. The object of the game is for
Adam to try to catch Eve. He calls out 'Where are you,
Eve?' and she must reply immediately 'Here I am, Adam'.
Adam goes towards her and she dodges him. He keeps
calling 'Where are you, Eve?' and she has to keep on
replying, straightaway 'Here I am, Adam'. Adam has to
catch her within a time limit of thirty seconds.

2 MENTAL GAMES

The Hobbies Game

The boys and girls form a circle and each concentrates
on the initials of their first name and surname. The
object is to make up an imaginary hobby with the same
set of initials

e.g. Martin Phillips   — Murmuring Poetry
   Ray Burdis   — Ringing Bells
   Dawn Gerron   — Drawing Giraffes
   Michael Scott   — Marvellous Singing
   Kim Taylforth   — Kissing Teddybears
   John Williams   — Just Work
   Jennifer Brassett — Judging Boys
   Gary Kemp   — Gliding Kites

Then they can make up hobbies for each other's initials. Licence is essential.

Lists and Word Tennis

Lists. This can be competitive or otherwise. Each contestant has just one minute to name all the items he can think of from a given category, e.g. Fruit, Vegetables, Cities, Countries, Meals, Girls' Names, Boys' Names, Clothes, Parts of the Body, Cars. So, if the category were Meals, he would start off: 'Sausages and Mash, Fish and Chips, Steak Pie, Baked Beans on Toast . . .' and continue until he runs out of ideas or the minute is up.

Word Tennis. A development of Lists is Word Tennis. Two people face each other and both have to name in turn items from the given category. They go on until one of them cannot think of a new word within three seconds; he is out and someone else can then challenge the winner.

A harder version of Word Tennis is to take words from a given category — 'Countries', for example—and specify that the last letter of one word must be the first letter of the next, e.g. 'EnglanD', 'DenmarK', 'KenyA', 'AustraliA' . . . . This form of Word Tennis is not so fast-moving, so a longer time limit is called for.

Kim's Game or the Memory Test

Take fifteen items (any selection of props — a comb, doll,

telephone, flowers, etc.) and place them on a tray. The contestant has one whole minute to concentrate hard on the items — and then the tray is taken away. He is given another minute to see how many of the items he can recall.

The number of items used can vary according to the age of the child. We suggest fifteen items for children of eleven to thirteen; you can increase or decrease the number according to age and ability.

One Minute Please

In this game the competitor sits in the hot seat and talks for one whole minute on a given subject, which can be more or less anything (sausages, football, television, girls, boys, holidays, school, parents, food, parties, etc.).

The object is for the child to learn to speak fluently for one minute without drying up or wandering off the subject. This will provide an opportunity to comment on the importance of increasing your vocabulary, good presentation, etc.

For younger children you can make this 'Thirty Seconds Please'.

Greetings, Your Majesty

One child is selected to be 'It' and sits on a chair at one end of the room, blindfolded. Then the teacher points at someone who walks to the middle and in a disguised voice says 'Greetings, Your Majesty' or another set phrase. 'It' has to try and guess whose voice it is; he is given two chances. If he guesses correctly he remains 'It'. If 'It' doesn't guess who it is, then the child has done a good job at disguising his voice and he becomes 'It', and so on.

Who Am I?

The subject sits in front of the class; the object of the game is for them to question him and guess what person he is thinking of. The subject can only answer 'Yes' or 'No' and you can stipulate that there should be only twenty questions. Because of this the class will not wish to waste any questions.

Example:
Q. 'Are you alive today?' A. 'Yes.'
Q. 'Are you a woman?' A. 'No.'
Q. 'Are you well known to the public?' A. 'Yes.'
Q. 'Are your a politician?' A. 'No.'
Q. 'Are you over thirty?' A. 'Yes.'
Q. 'Are you English?' A. 'No.'
Q. 'Are you European?' A. 'No.'
Q. 'Are you American?' A. 'Yes.'
Q. 'Are you a film star?' A. 'No.'
Q. 'Do you appear on television?' A. 'Yes.'
Q. 'Are you a singer?' A. 'No.'
Q. 'Are you involved in any way in sport?' A. 'Yes.'
Q. 'Are you a tennis player?' A. 'No.'
Q. 'Are you a boxer?' A. 'Yes.'
Q. 'Are you black?' A. 'Yes.'
Q. 'Are you Muhammad Ali?' A. 'Yes.'

The audience can be broken down into teams and you could see which team takes the least number of questions to find the answer to 'Who am I?'

TWO

The Spoken Word

1 SPEAKEASY

This is a good introduction to discussions and because it is conducted in an orderly way, everyone gets a chance to have their say, be it short or long. (The title is taken from Jimmy Savile's BBC radio programme.)

Place a chair at one end of the room; this is the Speakeasy chair. Announce a speakeasy subject—for example, 'If I had £100'. Each person in turn comes out to the Speakeasy chair and starts 'If I had £100 I would . . .'

This naturally introduces the importance of projection and also good listening, so that the whole class can hear what each person has to say.

Here is a list of Speakeasy titles for all ages:

Hobbies and collections.
My mum.
My dad.
My family.
My teacher/describe a teacher.
If I had £100.
If I ruled the world.
If I were an M.P.
If I had one wish/three wishes
The gift I'd choose for . . . (you can choose a gift for someone in the class or outside e.g. 'The gift I'd choose for Tommy Pender is a football because he's always borrowing mine' or 'The gift I'd choose for the Prime Minister is some throat pastilles so he won't get a sore throat from all the speeches he makes.' It's important to explain the reason for each gift.)
The gift I'd like to receive.
If Jesus was born today, the gift I would give him.
The best present I received/gave.
Wedding presents.
Complaints about home/family.
Complaints about school.
My happiest moment.
My saddest moment.

28

My funniest moment.

Memorable moments.

Magic moments. (Have you had a magic moment that has stuck in your mind, like the time you found the teacher's purse when everyone was desperately looking for it, or the time you saw some kittens being born?)

My holiday.

If I didn't live where I do, where I'd like to live and why.

If I wasn't born human, the animal I'd be and why.

If I wasn't born me, the person I'd be and why.

If my house was on fire, what I'd save and why. (Make it understood that all the human beings and animals have already been saved.)

The most beautiful thing in life.

The most ugly thing in life.

What makes me mad.

Myself.

A day from my diary.

The time I had to say goodbye to someone/something.

Reunions.

What I'll do when I grow up and why.

The job I'd like to have and why.

The job I'd hate to have and why.

How I see myself in ten years time.

The film/book I liked and why.

Description of a film.

Description of a book, or the book I am reading.

The programme/advertisement I like best/least on television and why.

Somebody nice that I like. (Straight description.)

The person I admire and why.

The person I'd like to meet and why.

Compliments. (A compliment is made to someone in the class: 'I'd like to compliment Tilly Vosburgh because she is always so sweet-natured a and helpful.' Tilly replies 'Thank you'. It doesn't have to be limited to people in the class.)

My favourite meal/my ideal menu.

The food I dislike and why.

In the box . . . . (Get the Speakeasy participant to close his eyes when he sits on the Speakeasy chair and imagine a box and its contents; after a short time ask what is in the box . . . .)

A letter to a friend.

How did you have that accident? (This is an imaginary accident, not a real one, but the answers, though they may be funny, must strike at plausibility.)

About the dentist. (Describe your feelings about visiting the dentist and what you like and dislike about it.)

If I were marooned on a desert island, the person I'd like to be with and why.
Tell-a-joke.

The following Speakeasy Titles are suitable for older groups:

What I like about myself.
What I don't like about myself.
The qualities I haven't got.
Decisions. (Have you had any difficult decisions to make? Indecision is an unhappy state but did you make the right choice? Describe a decision.)
The crossroads of my life.
My most embarrasing moment.
The thing that hurt me.
Near misses.
If only . . . (The object of this quick Speakeasy is to start with the words 'If only . . .'. For example, 'If only I had a car, then I wouldn't have to walk to school'. 'If only I wasn't so bad-tempered, then I'd get on better with my sister.' They must state the consequence of their 'If only . . .'
Phobias.

My obituary.
The prize for . . . goes to . . . . (This can be either funny or straight. 'The prize for corny jokes goes to Keith Johnson. The prize for always being late goes to Ray Burdis.' It doesn't have to be limited to people in the class: 'The prize for not being amused goes to Queen Victoria.')
Love is . . . .
Puppy love. (The first time I fell in love.)
The sort of boy/girl I find attractive.
The girl/boy I'd like to marry. (The idea is not to name names but rather describe the qualities of the person you'd like to be your husband or wife.)
If I had a T-shirt with a message or slogan on it, what it would be and why.

2 DISCUSSION

The Speakeasy is a good introduction to discussion as it prepares the ground for treatment in depth of larger subjects. Signals like hands-up are useful because other-

wise it is easy for the discussion to get out of control.
A strong chairman, probably the teacher, is essential
except in a very small group.

A variation of a discussion is 'Any Questions' in
which, as in the BBC radio programme, there is a panel
of about four people and questions are put by members
of the class, asking the panel their views on matters of
topical interest.

Here are some discussion themes:

Parents and family.	Newspapers.
School (co-education or single sex, school uniform, etc.)	Topical and current affairs.
	The monarchy.
Your local environment.	Good and bad manners.
Money.	Prejudice.
Religion.	Consumer questions.
Morals.	Preferences in the content of
Television and Radio.	drama lessons and new ideas.

3 STORIES, SOUNDS AND SPEAKING

Sound circle

The boys and girls form a circle and each in turn makes
a sound from a given category. For example, you may
ask for sound effects (a cork, creaking door, puffing up
a tyre, an electric train, a racing car, escaping gas, factory
hooter), or animal noises; a sentence in a dialect; names
and emotions (saying your own name angrily, sadly,
boredly, fearfully . . .); voice patterns (making a sound
pattern out of your own name, or with the name of a
city, like chanting Lon-don Lon-don to the tune of Big
Ben); variety of sound (any sound which the human voice
can make); speech inflexions (take a word or phrase like
'Yes', 'No' 'Thank you' or 'Hello, how are you?' Pass it
round the sound circle and see how much variety there
can be in modulation, pitch, tone and dialect); echoes

(one begins 'Are you feeling all right?', the second person
repeats the same phrase, imitating the voice, accent and
tone of the first as precisely as possible, the third person
chooses a new phrase, 'Phew, it's hot in here', said in
whatever way he wishes, which is in turn imitated by the
fourth. Go round twice so that everyone starts one phrase
and echoes one phrase).

Within the sound circle you can play guessing games
such as 'What's My Sound Effect?' and 'What's My
Dialect?'.

Stories-all-sorts

Making up a story as they go along is something many
children are very good at: improvising on the spot gets
round the 'writing it down' barrier.

Three props on a box. Select three props—say, a
telephone, an iron and a newspaper—and place them on
a box. Someone comes out and makes up a story
bringing in the telephone, the iron and the newspaper.

For *one-minute stories* three or more children sit in
front of the class and, on request, close their eyes. You
give them a theme — 'The Body' — and each has to name
one part of the body — the first child thinks perhaps of
the arm, the second thinks of the heart and the third of
the elbow. Then the first child is asked to tell a story
called 'The Arm', the second 'The Heart' and the third
'The Elbow'. The stories are to be about one minute long.
Other umbrella themes for one-minute stories include
'Food', 'Clothes', 'Other Countries', 'Animals'. In each
case the teacher asks the storytellers to close their eyes
and think of . . . 'a kind of food' . . . 'what food are you
thinking of?', etc.

Bell stories are a sharpening-up exercise for the more
advanced storyteller. He begins to tell a story but as soon
as the bell sounds he has to break off and start a new

story until the bell goes again. Each time the bell rings a new story is started, until the storyteller has started five or six stories. The teacher may ring the bell after two seconds, or he may decide to stay with one story for half a minute or more. *Bell letters* work on the same principle.

What does the music mean to you?

The class listens to a piece of music with eyes closed, and then one by one the children describe what they saw in their mind's eye while listening to the music. Any kind of music can be chosen.

Carry-on-story, etc.

The *carry-on-story* is what its name suggests. Four or five people take part each time. The teacher or first person starts off the story, talking for about half a minute and passing it on to the next person by the link work 'and . . .'. The last person finishes the story. The carry-on-story can also be started by the teacher announcing a title ('The Black Cat', 'Pancakes').

The *one-word-story* has two or more participants. They supply alternate words, going quickly backwards and forwards and making up a complete story. Listening and co-operation are very important. A one-word-story can either be told straight or acted out, as it is told, which is more difficult.

One-sentence-story takes place with a circle of people each supplying a single sentence in turn to form the story. Again, the listening is very important.

Finish-the-story is a variation of the carry-on-story. Two or three people go out of the room. They come back in one by one and the teacher or someone else starts off a story in the same way for each of them, which they have to finish in their own way. It's interesting to see how the stories may differ.

Other ways of doing stories are to give the storyteller a title, a first line, or a last line to use.

Letters, telegrams and cards

The idea of this is to improvise writing a letter you are going to send to a friend, your aunt, the teacher, or to apply for a job;

or to read aloud a letter you've just received — the teacher can specify that it must contain good news or bad news, or be a newsy family letter, or an official letter, etc.;

or the boys and girls form a circle and each improvise reading a telegram:

BOUNCING BABY BOY BOTH WELL SYD

FATHER ILL COME HOME IMMEDIATELY STOP
      MOTHER

BIRTHDAY GREETINGS LOVE HEATHER AND
      DAVE

or each can improvise a card: either a thank-you card, a picture post card, a Christmas card, a birthday card, a get well soon card, congratulations (on a wedding, birth of a baby, passing exams or driving test), or any other kind of card.

From morning till now

This is a detailed monologue in which each person describes what they have done that day from when they awoke in the morning to the present moment.

If desired, you can extend this by asking questions. What was the best thing that happened today? the worst? the most interesting? did they use their time well?

This is not the 'Truth Game'. It might be an idea to reassure everyone at the start that they are not going to be asked to reveal any secrets!

Interviews

To start with, the teacher can be the interviewer and
each child in turn can be interviewed. It can be a straight
interview or a simulation of an interview for a new
school or for a job. This is good practice for the future.
The importance of punctuality, tidiness and clear speech
can be brought home here.

Standard questions include:

'What are your hobbies?'
'What do you like doing best at school?'
'Will you tell me about your brothers and sisters?'
'How many people are there in your school?'
'What books do you like reading?'
'Why do you want to come to this school?'/Why do you
want this job?'

The interviewer and interviewee can exchange roles and
after the interview they can comment constructively on
how they think each other did.

Social procedures can be dealt with in the same way
as interviews. For example, ordering a meal in a
restaurant, booking a hotel room, making a complaint —
and how best to get your way when you do so.

The Newscaster

This is quite a difficult piece of work as the Newcaster
must not hesitate while reading the news, but must
remain completely neutral and impassive — it's really
an exercise in fluency and self-control.

The Newscaster sits at his desk and improvises the
reading of three realistic news items (you can specify
more). He must not pause or stumble — the aim is to be
as articulate as possible.

On similar lines, you can ask for a radio or TV

commentary (specify which) on a sports event such as the Grand National or the Cup Final. For realism, care must be taken to be accurate with the technicalities of the particular sport; they should also perhaps be given licence to send it up.

Make friends, argue

Group the class into pairs at random and ask each pair to talk to each other, making friends; they do so until 'freeze'. Then you can possibly ask one pair to continue their conversation for everybody to listen to. Then everyone talks in their pairs again but this time their brief is to have an argument: after 'freeze' you can again spotlight one pair. Then everyone finds a new partner and continues to make friends – argue – make friends – argue.

This is a very good verbal warm-up.

The five senses

'Sight, sound, touch, taste and smell – we see with our eyes, we hear with our ears, we touch with our skin, we taste with the taste buds on our tongue and we smell with out nose . . . .' You can continue with a preamble on a blind man's use of the white stick, braille, etc., evoking sensitivity and awareness of the five senses.

Select five children: one is sight, one sound, one touch, one taste, and one smell. Ask each in turn to say:

Sight: What he'd love to see and what he'd hate to see.

Sound: What he'd love to hear and what he'd hate to hear.

Touch: What he'd love to touch and what he'd hate to touch.

Taste: What he'd love to taste and what he'd hate to taste.

Smell: What he'd love to smell and what he'd hate to smell.

4 WORD GAMES

Opposites Game

Select one child as 'It' and another (it can be two others) as the Questioner. The Questioner can ask any questions he chooses which have a yes/no answer and 'It' may only answer 'Yes' or 'No'. If the Questioner asks 'It' 'Are you a human being?', the answer is 'No' for in the Opposites Game you must give the *opposite* to the true answer.

e.g. Questions asked to John Blundell:

Q. 'Is your name John Blundell?' A. 'No.'
Q. 'Are you a girl?' A. 'Yes.'
Q. 'Did you brush your teeth with boot polish this morning?' A. 'Yes.'
Q. 'Have you got eight fingers?' A. 'No.'

If 'It' fails to give a correct opposite, or does not answer a question within five seconds, he is out. If he can survive for a minute, he wins.

If you want to make it even harder, another rule that 'It' may not laugh can be added.

Yes/No Game

The Questioner must be a skilled fast talker for the Yes/No Game. The contestant is led to the hot seat and is bombarded with a series of questions to which he must not answer 'Yes' or 'No' or nod or shake his head — but of course he must answer immediately. Needless to say, all questions are directed towards a yes/no answer like 'Do you go to school? Do you smoke? Did you watch tv last night? Are you married? Have you got brothers and sisters?'

If the contestant survives one minute of the ordeal, he is declared the winner.

Fortunately, unfortunately

The boys and girls form a circle. One starts off 'Fortunately I was on time for school today', the next continues 'But unfortunately the teacher told me off for not doing my homework', next 'But fortunately she soon forgot about me because at that moment the Headmaster came into the room', 'But unfortunately when he went out she took away my break', 'But fortunately it didn't really matter because just then a flying saucer flew past the window' . . . and so on.

Each alternate 'fortunately, unfortunately' must be consistent with the meaning of the story. No *non sequiturs*.

This can be developed into an elimination game. Any hesitation, repetition or *non sequitur* and you are out. To make it really hard, you can also forbid simple opposites (e.g. 'Unfortunately I lost my money', 'Fortunately I found it again').

The Minister's Cat

The boys and girls form a circle, either seated or standing. A rhythmical clap of four beats begins and the first person starts with the first letter of the alphabet: 'The minister's cat's an *angry* cat', clap, clap, clap, clap, and the next continues 'The minister's cat's an *ancient* cat', clap, clap, clap, clap, 'The minister's cat's an *artistic* cat', clap, clap, clap, clap, and on it goes. The first person unable to think of a new adjective or missing the beat drops out of the circle and so the next round begins, starting with the next letter of the alphabet, and the game gradually goes faster as it continues.

Sausage

The object of this game is for the contestant not to
laugh when answering 'Sausage' to each of the questions
asked. To put it in theatrical terms — there must be no
corpsing!

Appoint a child to sit on the hot seat:

Q. 'What's your name?' A. 'Sausage.'
Q. 'What's that in the middle of your face?'
   A. 'Sausage.'
Q. 'What is the Head of this school called?'
   A. 'Sausage.'
Q. 'Now, dear, look down at the floor — what are
   you wearing on your feet?' A. 'Sausage.'
Q. 'What did you have for breakfast?' A. 'Sausage.'
Q. 'Before you go to bed tonight, what will you
   brush your teeth with?' A. 'Sausage.'

If the appointed child survives ten questions with a
completely straight face, he's done very well!

Story charades

This is a variation of ordinary charades. One person tells
three different stories. In story number one he brings
in the first half of the word, in story number two the
second half of the word is brought in, and story number
three includes the complete word. The class endeavour
to guess the word at the end. No hands go up in the
middle of the story charades.

The Metaphors Game

For this you need a panel with about three members,
and a popular member of the class is chosen to be the
subject. The subject sits in front of the panel who
describe him by means of the metaphor: what animal

would the subject be if he were an animal? What colour would he be if he were a colour? What kind of food? What make of car? What record? What tv or film character? Article of clothing? What name, other than his own would he have? And so on.

THREE

Warm-ups, Mime and Movement

1 WARM-UPS

Each drama session begins with a warm-up.

The aim of this is to relax everybody, mentally and physically, and reduce any inhibitions they may have.

During the warm-up the class concentrates. A positive start helps everyone to get down to work in a business-like way.

Warm-up exercises

The children find a space, then stretch their arms out and swing them to make sure they won't hit each other. Either the teacher or a member of the class can lead the warm-up exercises.

Start warming up by shaking all over in time to some lively music (although music is not essential), rub the hands together and slap them all over the body. Continue with head movements, nodding up and down and turning from side to side, then rotate the head all the way round and all the way back, to relax the neck. Repeat. Shoulders next. Shrug shoulders up and down, then right shoulder, left shoulder alternately. Swing hips from side to side, rotate the pelvic girdle and stretch the trunk forwards, backwards and sideways.

Go right down to a squat position, with heels on the floor if possible, and up again. Repeat this several times. Stretch the arms as high as possible, growing at least two inches taller; jump up and down on the spot, leaping higher and higher, and then shake all over again. These simple warm-up exercises can be supplemented by floor exercises: cycling with legs in the air, making scissors movements and so on.

Curl and stretch — relaxing

The children start off by curling up in a tight little ball, as small as possible, on the floor. To a background of soothing music they gradually uncurl, get up and stretch until their legs, backs and necks are stretched and their arms, hands and fingertips completely extended upwards. Then they start again from the curled position and work upwards once more until their entire bodies are completely stretched. This is repeated until the music finishes, when the children stretch out on the floor. The teacher tells them to flop completely, relaxing their heads, bodies and limbs as if they were asleep. They can be given the 'relaxation test' by lifting a hand or foot a few inches to feel if it is tense or not; it should be completely floppy. Don't drop their hand on the floor as, if they are relaxing really well, it will hurt. Lay it down gently.

Dance patterns and follow-my-leader

The class stands in a circle. The teacher goes to the centre of the circle and starts a simple and repetitive dance pattern to a strong rhythm (e.g. clicking fingers followed by marching steps). The boys and girls pick up the dance pattern until the teacher calls 'Freeze'; leaders from the class are then invited to start off new dance patterns in turn, separating each by the magic word 'Freeze'. Dance patterns can be done to music with a strong beat, a drum or other percussion, or to a clapping rhythm.

The dance pattern can also be done follow-my-leader style round the room and on 'Freeze' the leader changes the dance pattern.

Runabout

Everyone finds a space and when the teacher says
'Action' they run round the room without bumping into
each other, dodging in and out. At 'Freeze' they stop
absolutely still. The exercise is repeated, but this time
on 'Action' they run backwards, again without bumping
into each other. Several repeats forwards and backwards
will provide a good warm-up to a session, for any age-
group.

The rope-hauling mime

This is a warm-up in which the group haul on imaginary
ropes in strong dance rhythm, with or without music.

Pull the rope down from the ship's mast, tugging on
it repeatedly. Then heave the rope from the side; lasso
it, whirling it round your head and throwing it into the
distance. Then haul it back in, feeling the strain in your
hands, your face and your body while you are pulling it
in. Tie it up in a knot. Then wind it rhythmically round
your elbow. Then have a tug-of-war in pairs, one partner
staggering forward as the other pulls the rope backward.
Finally, pull the ropes down from the mast and heave
from the side again.

In a class situation the teacher leads the children in
the movements and calls out the changes. Tell the class
to feel the rope's strength and texture in their hands
while they do the mime.

Instruments of the orchestra

Start by inviting the children to name as many instru-
ments of the orchestra as they can think of. This is an
opportunity to bring in general knowledge about the
families of the orchestra—string, woodwind, brass and
percussion—the conductor and his baton, famous
composers and what they wrote, etc.

Then, to any suitable orchestral or band music, let
them mime each instrument in detail, e.g. when playing
the piano, make sure they don't forget the pedal, and
the left hand turning the page of the music. The teacher
calls out each instrument to be mimed in turn: violin,
flute, trombone, guitar, xylophone, cymbals, drums, and
so on, not forgetting the conductor and singers, if
appropriate.

Alternatively, you can divide the group up into
sections, each section playing a given instrument and
following the part of that instrument in the music.

Drums mime

This is another musical idea for younger children, in
which they sit or stand in front of an entire imaginary
drumkit, including bass drum and cymbal, and, accom-
panied by a suitable record, play in jazz or pop-drummer
style, putting in such flashy details as throwing the
stick under the leg and into the air and catching it. From
time to time throughout the piece of music, the teacher
can call out 'Spotlight on Martin Kemp', for example,
whereupon Martin takes his solo, playing with great
energy and concentration while the other drummers drop
on one knee and extend one hand towards the soloist to
give a spotlighting effect. At the end of the solo the call
is 'And . . . everybody' and all the players pick up their
drumming again.

Mambo Mamba and other dances

Mambo Mamba. This is good fun. The mambo is the
dance, the mamba is the snake. The children are going
to make a mamba out of the mambo. What you do is
a mambo-type dance with the teacher leading to start
with, picking two or three more children to join in on
each circuit, making a snakelike pattern across the floor.

At the last step of each phrase the head is jerked forward and the bottom pushed back and the feet lift slightly off the floor. Simultaneously, you make a fairly high-pitched 'Ooh' sound. Listen to 'Florida Fantasy' from the *Midnight Cowboy* LP and you'll get the idea. For all ages.

We don't propose to go into dance in great detail but would like to suggest its value in warm-ups. Apart from the Mambo, the Charleston and Cha-Cha-Cha are equally good starting-off points for a drama session, and to be topical you could include Irish jigs and reels on St Patrick's Day (17th March), or the Highland Fling on St Andrew's Day (30th November), and various other national and folk dances. Dances from different historical periods, c.g. Elizabethan, are another field that can be explored.

Snowball

This makes a session end on a high note for any age group. Select a good dancing record from the top twenty (the children will often bring in their own). Someone starts dancing with a partner and then on cue (you can use a football rattle, a whistle or a bell, or simply call out 'Change'), they double up, each picking a new partner and continue dancing till the next change. Eventually you call out 'Everybody dancing' so there will be no wallflowers.

2 MOVEMENT

Marching, skipping and other ways of moving round the room

Marching. This is very simple and a guaranteed winner with younger children. Pick a leader who begins a rousing march round the acting area in time to appropriate music. On each circuit he picks two or three more children to march round behind him in follow-my-leader style until eventually all the children are marching round one behind the other, swinging their arms, heads high or high-stepping like drum-majorettes.

The leader can march and countermarch them in S-shaped patterns all over the room until the music finishes.

Skipping. This is as simple as marching. One child starts off, picks a partner, and together they skip round the room. At the call of 'Change' the partners split up and each finds another partner to go on with. 'Change' again and all four choose new partners and so on until there are eight couples skipping round, or, in a large room, sixteen. Then the call is 'And back to your places', and someone else starts it off again, building up once more, until the end of the record. You will need music with a syncopated, skipping rhythm.

Other ways of moving round the room. Number the children 'one, two, three and four, one, two, three and four . . .' and tell all the 'ones' to go round the room in a specified way and then back to their places; the 'twos' continue with a different movement, followed by the 'threes' and then the 'fours'. There are many ways of moving round the room; here are some of them:

Silly walks; hopping; jumping; athlete's walk; walking backwards; moon-walking; running in slow motion; footballers training; skating; crawling; cartwheels; limps; clown's caper; creeping; tap-dancing; on tiptoe; heel walking; high kicking; as an old man; like a person in a hurry; as a Dalek; carrying a heavy bag; happily; miserably; proudly; lazily; drunkenly; ambling; like a mouse, an elephant, a horse, circus horses; through autumn leaves; and barefoot across shingle.

This can be done with all ages, using movements appropriate to each age group. Chirpy, energetic music is best.

Running

The children find a space and, to the accompaniment of fast music, start running on the spot with everyone putting lots of energy into it: then, while still running on the spot, they reach out to grab something — but it's always just out of reach. Next, they are running away, being chased in a nightmare, but their legs are carrying them no further than that same spot. Still they keep on running on the spot but now they are each an exhausted long distance runner; then, with a great spurt of energy they run with knees up, training for fitness. End with a triumphant lap of honour waving to the crowd. Khachaturian's 'Sabre Dance' is good for this.

Swimming

Invite the children to suggest all the swimming strokes; breast stroke, overarm, butterfly, back stroke, dog paddle. In time with music the children mime each stroke in turn as instructed by the teacher, starting by working on the spot and then changing to everyone going round the room in the same direction.

Ball games

The boys and girls find a space and begin by juggling with an imaginary ball, keeping their eyes on it. Then the ball becomes a beach ball which they bounce high and low; it becomes a big, heavy ball for bowling at a bowling alley; it is used for shooting in netball and then for bowling in cricket; then they play catch in pairs and play ball against the wall by themselves, or play basketball — or they can mime whatever ball game they like.

Other sports can be mimed to music by the teacher simply calling out the name of the sport — tennis, cricket, football, etc. The miming of the sports can be carried out in slow-motion as in an action replay, as well.

Boxing with an imaginary person

This is mainly for the boys. They find a space and box with an imaginary person, paying attention to strong punching movements, foot work, head and body reactions and knockdowns. They start as a group and on the teacher's request go back to their places. Individuals are called out to demonstrate their skills. They finish as a group again.

Kung Fu and James Bond type fighting, again with an imaginary person, is as cathartic and energetic as the boxing.

Theme music from film and television thrillers will give you the right atmosphere.

The Chase

In this, the secret agent shadows the villain, or the killer stalks his victim, through a dramatic landscape represented by stage blocks, screens, ramps, and over-turned chairs and tables; creeping round corners, leaping over walls, diving for cover, and so on, their tracks criss-crossing the acting area, the pursued always keeps one jump ahead of the pursuer.

For maximum effect, the participants must give each other room to work in: the idea is not to simply have one person chasing another around the room, so the pursuer must not get too close to the pursued.

Stylized movements — pirouettes, karate chops, Kung Fu, somersaults, stunt-man stage falls, can be brought in to give the chase extra excitement.

One possible dénouement is to have the victim reach

a telephone and start to summon help on it, only to be gunned down, stabbed or strangled by his or her pursuer, ending with a bloodcurdling scream.

Guns, dark glasses and sinister-looking hats are useful props for this. Thriller/suspense type music and shadowy lighting help to set the scene.

The Hands Dance

This is a very simple idea for younger children. The children make their hands dance, expressing the feeling of the music by making improvised abstract movements in the air. After a while, more specific actions can be introduced, e.g. representing a butterfly by linking the thumbs and fluttering the fingers, or waving goodbye, or moving the hands together as if in prayer, or sewing, conducting, or playing the piano.

The Legs Dance

This is the same as the Hands Dance, but using legs instead of hands, so there is not such a great variety of possible movements. To start with, the class lie flat on their backs with their legs in the air and move them in a slow, single rhythm, and then in a fast, double rhythm, bicycling and making scissors movements both forwards and sideways. This can be repeated several times, slow and fast. Then they can do their own improvised movements, in time with slow, rhythmic music.

Mirror-images

This can be done by all ages. The class divides into pairs and, kneeling down facing one another, make movements in time with the music, one being the leader and the other following the same movements exactly, like a reflection in a mirror, i.e. moving the left hand to correspond with the other person's right and so on. Either improvised abstract patterns can be used or else the intricate movements of brushing the teeth and combing the hair; washing; for boys, shaving; and, for girls, doing their make-up. The whole exercise can be repeated with the leader and the reflection exchanging roles.

Machines

One member of the group starts making a repetitive machine-like action, strong and stiff, over and over again. He can stand on one spot and move his arms round jerkily, or perhaps take three steps forward and three steps back, or lie on the ground lifting alternate feet in the air, or make any other movement that comes into his head, in time with the music.

Others are picked to join in, one by one, adding their mechanical actions to the machine that is being built up, using different levels: standing, sitting, kneeling or lying down, continuing until the teacher, or leader calls 'Freeze', and immediately restarting on 'Action'. The idea is for the children to join in where they will fit in best with the parts of the machine that are already there. After the music stops, the teacher calls 'Freeze' and instructs the machine to continue on 'Action', but making machine-like noises.

Later on, you can adjust the machine to operate in slow-motion with half-speed sounds and actions, and then in rapid-motion with double speed and sound, again using the words 'Freeze' and 'Action'.

With a large group you can build up two or three machines at the same time, instead of one enormous machine. Jerky, West Indian rhythms are ideal for this.

Space Creatures

Divide the children into groups of sixes and sevens. How

would they imagine a space creature? Each group makes
a composite space creature with their bodies, not
forgetting suitable facial expressions. They can either be
mobile or stationary. Then follows a space creature
parade, with the stationary ones in the middle, and the
mobile ones moving round them, to eerie, science-fiction
music, like that from the film *2001*, or weird sound effects
effects such as those produced by the Moog synthesizer.

The Sculptor and the Statue

Everyone finds a partner and they sit on the ground
together. For young children, you can explain the
difference between a sculptor and a sculpture. Without
talking, each sculptor must mould his partner into a
sculpture. It can be grotesque or beautiful. As an
example, the teacher can pick someone to be his own
sculpture, shaping the head, moulding the face, eyes
open or closed, fixing the expression, positioning arms,
legs and body. When the music begins the children set
to work on their own sculptures. After a couple of
minutes, the teacher fades out the music and asks the
sculptors to go back to their places in the audience.
The statues remain where they are. Fade in the music
again as the sculptors from their seats observe all the
statues. Fade out the music and invite comments, or
ask for titles for the statues. Tell the statues to go
round the room in their shapes and characters, first
slowly and then quickly — fade in the music for this.
    Then the children can change partners, the sculptors
becoming sculptures and vice versa.
    A variation of this is 'The Spooky Garden', in which
the sculptors make really grotesque statues and then
two or three children wander among them, exploring
'the spooky garden'.
    Another variation is 'What's my statue?', when,

again working in twos, one partner makes a statue of the other as an occupation, e.g. pop singer, teacher, dentist, and invites the class to guess 'What's my statue?'

Background music such as Peer Gynt 'Hall of the Mountain King' (Grieg) is very effective; also electronic music.

A more advanced idea, in which people work individually, is 'Titles and Statues'. Each person announces his title, which may be abstract, topical, humorous or a well-known person, whatever they like, and then forms himself into the shape of the sculpture with that title. If mood music is used it is interesting to see how it affects the character of the statues produced.

A similar idea is 'The Artist and the Painting'. One artist is appointed to make a picture with a group of four or five. He announces the title and then steps into the picture himself.

A further development of this is for the artist to make the picture and then to tell the story that the picture illustrates.

Snake and Snake-Charmer

The children find a partner and sit on the ground. One is the snake the other the snake-charmer. The snake-charmers sit cross-legged, playing their flutes to coax their snakes to dance. The snakes, making themselves as small as possible, cup their hands in front of them to represent the head of the snake and make snake-like wriggling movements, twisting and turning to the music. After a while the snakes and snake-charmers exchange roles.

Indian music with sitars or flutes, can be used for this.

A dance drama: Under the Sea

Get the children to name as many creatures that live

under the sea as possible: fish, crabs, octopuses, sea anemones, etc.

From this you can develop a fantasy piece with King Neptune standing on a stage block in the centre of the arena. Around Neptune lie the underwater creatures, sleeping to begin with: a group of fish in one corner, four or six sea anemones in pairs with arms and legs entwined, nearby a couple of upturned crabs, two beautiful mermaids and half a dozen or so fat octopuses. Some dreamy music starts, Neptune comes down from his abode and wakes up the creatures in turn. On awakening they start to move: the fish darting to and fro, high and low amongst the other sea creatures; the sea anemones, all arms and legs, swaying from side to side and round and round; the upturned crabs wriggling their arms and legs; the two beautiful mermaids combing their long tresses in mirror-images; and the fat octopuses clumping around in their corner. Neptune can perhaps wave a trident or a scarf over the water creatures to awaken them. As the music finishes, the water creatures return to their starting positions and adopt the same sleeping poses as before, while Neptune goes back and stands high on his rock.

There are several other dance dramas that can be adapted using suitable music, such as the story of Samson and Delilah set to 'The Good, the Bad and the Ugly'; a tribal dance set to one of the sections of the 'Missa Luba'; dolls (teddy bear, jack-in-the-box, clockwork soldiers, clowns, etc.) coming to life in the attic, set to 'Puppet on a String'. Then there are many songs with a story that immediately lends itself to mime; for example 'Little White Bull'; 'Goodness Gracious Me'; 'Seven Little Girls Sitting in the Back Seat'; 'Cinderella Rockefella'; 'Tubby the Tuba'; 'The Sorcerers Apprentice'.

Good atmospheric music, like Grieg's 'In the Hall of
the Mountain King' and Handel's 'Arrival of the Queen
of Sheba', is bound to conjure up ideas for the children
to make up their own dance dramas.

More experienced boys and girls can bring in their
own music and work out mime and improvisation ideas
based upon it.

The Man-eating Plant

Dance dramas can be done to a combination of story and
music as well as to music alone; for example, 'The Man-
Eating Plant'. Everyone sits on the floor and the story
begins, to the accompaniment of dramatic music.

'You are a traveller in a far-off land, the weather is
very hot and you have been walking since seven o'clock
in the morning. Now it is lunchtime and you lie down
exhausted in the shade of a big plant with large green
leaves . . . you are eating the sandwiches you have
brought with you . . . you finish off the last bite of the
last sandwich . . . and screw up the paper into a ball and
put it back tidily in your knapsack . . . and now you
begin to feel really sleepy . . . and you lean back against
the stem of the plant with your eyes half closed . . . and
then, out of the corner of your eye, you notice that,
although there is no wind, the branches of the plant are
slowly waving in the air and coming nearer and nearer
to you . . . and, too late, you realize it's a man-eating
plant, and it's got you in its grasp . . . and you struggle
against it . . . trying to fight off the branches . . . and
you're getting weaker and weaker . . . but then the plant
seems to give up the struggle, and its branches retreat . . .
that was a close shave . . . but it's coming back again . . .
and this time it finishes you off.'

While the story is being told the class improvise the
movements suggested by it.

Greeting each other in a new way

The Eskimos rub noses together. The English shake hands. The Russians kiss on either cheek. Frenchmen kiss a lady's hand. The children go into pairs and, to lively music, find a new way of greeting each other — perhaps they might even start a new fashion! When they've worked out their greeting action (it could be pulling each other's hair followed by two jumps, or it could be clapping hands on shoulders and doing a leapfrog), they go back to their places ready to show the teacher and class each greeting in turn. This can be done by all ages.

The Touch Game

In total silence, the class walk slowly around the room with their eyes closed. As soon as anyone senses some-one near them, they move out of that person's way without bumping into each other.

Then the teacher, who is the only one with his eyes open, asks everyone to reach out and find a partner. This they do; anyone who hasn't found a partner raises his hand and the teacher brings them into pairs. They do not open their eyes. The teacher tells them to feel each other's hands, the texture, the shape, the nails — are they sharp? Is it a hot hand? Is it a cold hand? Is it clammy? Shake hands. Clap each other's hands. Make friends with each others hands. Argue. Again make friends and argue with the hands. And . . . open your eyes! Everyone will enjoy this game — provided they don'it cheat by opening their eyes in the middle.

The teacher can link this with the five senses and how important the sense of touch is to the blind.

A similar exercise can be done using backs instead of hands.

3 MIME

Miming actions

Explain that mime is drama with actions but without
words, therefore the actions must be made very clearly;
so clearly, in fact, that if someone is miming sewing with
a needle and thread you want to, in effect, be able to see
that needle and thread!

The following actions can be mimed by all the class —
knitting, sewing, writing, playing the piano, lighting a
cigarette and smoking it, typing (putting the paper in
first), make-up including varnishing nails, or shaving,
peeling onions, sharpening a pencil, sugaring and stirring
tea, stroking a cat, polishing shoes, brushing teeth,
painting a picture, sweeping the floor, polishing the floor,
painting a door, cleaning the windows . . . .

This can be developed into more detailed mime such
as different ways of combing your hair: fussy and
nervous, backcombing, vain, bored, it's tangled, finding
dandruff on your shoulder . . .

The miming of eating different foods is fun: a banana,
chicken leg, apple, soup, spaghetti, orange, steak, boiled
egg, ice cream . . . and eating in different ways — slowly,
greedily, nervously, fussily, with the mouth open, made
to eat something you don't like, hurriedly, it's too hot,
chewing, something gets stuck in your throat, you're
preoccupied, reading the paper at the same time . . . .

The key point is concentration. For example, suppose
the class are miming painting a picture. Tell them to
visualize the half-finished picture in front of them: a
portrait, a landscape, or an abstract; ask them one by
one to describe their painting. If they are writing, what
are they writing? A letter, school work, a story? What
does it say? Are they writing with a pen or a pencil? And
so on.

You can go on to more detailed mime, including preparing a scrambled egg or omelette, making the tea, making a daisy chain.

Touch mime

This is a more complicated form of the miming actions idea and needs the right atmosphere to evoke the sensitivity required.

How does it feel?

Pat a dog; pull it back by its collar; it jumps up at you.

Pick up a heavy rock; throw it in a pool; wipe the grit off your hands.

Touch a polished oak table.

Put on a warm fur coat.

Walk barefoot down a stony beach; the water is freezing cold; now the sun comes out — enjoy it.

Pick up an apple; toss it in the air and catch it; feel the skin of the apple; smell its scent; take a bite and taste it.

You are asking the class not only to mime the actions, but also to recreate in their minds the sensations produced by them. This idea develops sensitivity and awareness.

Guess-the-mime (What's my job? etc.)

One person starts by announcing 'What's my job?' and begins to mime his job — a chef, teacher, mechanic, or whatever. On finishing the mime he asks again 'What's my job?' and the class guesses. If the mime is really good, they will get it right. (No hands go up in the middle of the mime — not until 'What's my job?' is said for the second time.) Then someone else has a turn; it could be the person who has guessed the previous job correctly.

Variations of this include 'What's my animal?', 'What's my sport?', 'What's my musical instrument?', and 'What's my circus character?'.

Mime charades is a more complicated guess-the-mime. The principle is the same as in ordinary charades but no words are spoken, of course. Words like 'window', 'monkey', 'football', 'carpet', and 'sandwich' are easily illustrated in a mime charade.

Take 'monkey': Act One (one finger raised in the air): Monk; a monk praying, the rosary, etc. Act Two (two fingers): Key; a key is taken from a pocket, turned in a lock and the door opened. Act Three (three fingers): Monkey; A monkey scampers around the room, swinging its arms, scratching itself and so on. Then the rest of the class have to guess the word.

Once a class have plenty of experience of mime, guess-the-mime as a group exercise is very enjoyable. The class divide into groups of about six and each mime a story from a given field, such as the Bible, Mythology or History. The audience guess-the-mime.

The Indefinite Prop and the Imaginary Prop

Take a prop — for example a carpet-beater — and place it in the middle of the floor. You want the children to use this as any object other than a carpet-beater. Each in turn uses the indefinite prop in a specific way — it could be a lollipop, a tennis racket, a frying pan, a mirror, a shovel, a sword and so on. The idea is firstly for them to use their imagination to think up more and more unlikely uses for the indefinite prop, and secondly for them to do a well-presented mime to illustrate what they have thought of. This can be done with any age-group.

The imaginary prop is similar to this except that you don't use an actual prop at all. The teacher can begin by eating an imaginary apple and then passing it to the person next to him. It now becomes a ball and is bounced on the floor before being passed along to the next person — now it is a hamster, which is being stroked — the person

after that sees it as a flower . . . . As the imaginary prop
is passed on, it is important to pay attention to the
detail of the mime in order to make it real for
everybody.

Animal walks

Number the children one, two, three and four, one, two,
three and four . . . . Put on some music and tell the
'ones' to be giraffes going round the room and returning
to their places, 'twos' monkeys, 'threes' mice, 'fours'
elephants – back to the 'ones' again and select new
animal walks – or even birds and fish.

'My animal is . . .' is a development of this where each
child individually chooses an animal and after announcing
what it is, does a mime of the animal, without music;
they can make the animal's sounds as well. This is not a
guessing game; the idea is for everyone to imagine what
it is like to be that particular kind of animal.

Reactions (football, etc.)

The children are spectators at a football match, either
watching the game live at the stadium or on television
(say which). The local team are playing against Leeds
United. You ask for their mimed reactions as the match
proceeds: 'We've scored; they've scored; we've got a goal
but the ref. says it's offside; a foul by us; a foul by
them; a penalty for us; a penalty for them; someone's
thrown a bottle on to the pitch; one of our players is
badly hurt; the ball's gone into the crowd and they
won't give it back.'

From the football pitch back to the class. Ask them
to sit in different ways concentrating on facial
expressions as well as whole body reactions. 'You are
dejected; you are embarrassed; excited; bored;
comfortable . . . .'

Other reactions of various kinds can be suggested by the teacher uttering short descriptive phrases: 'A bird falls from a wall, it is very bady hurt' — you feel pity; 'The postman brings a large parcel addressed to you' — surprise; 'From an upstairs window you see the boy next door throwing stones at your dog' — anger; 'You are at home alone at night and you hear a strange noise coming from upstairs' — fear, etc.

You can ask older age-groups to sit in different ways, concentrating on whole body reactions as well as facial expressions. Again, you will tell them the nature of each reaction involved, but you will leave it to each individual to create the reason for it in his own mind: 'You are feeling confident; you are embarrassed; excited; bored; in love . . . .'

The Goalkeeper

This is a good character mime which can be done individually or with a whole group.

The goalkeeper is standing in his goal and he mimes his reactions to the progress of the game. He is bored because play is all at the other end of the pitch. His team has scored a goal. Someone throws something from the crowd. Ready for a corner kick, he shouts (in mime) at the defenders. He makes a save. He goes for a high ball but is fouled in mid-air. The opponents score a goal. He shouts (in mime) to blame a defender. He picks up the ball from the back of the net.

Mime sketch: the four secretaries

Four attractive secretaries are sitting in front of their typewriters, typing busily. A plate glass window separates them from the street outside. A 'pick-up' of dubious character prowls outside the plate glass

window, raps on the glass and tries to get each girl
in turn to come outside. We see the reactions of each
girl as our man in the street tries his luck. He may be
successful or he may not!

FOUR

Characters, Props and Costumes

1 CHARACTERS

From the beginning, children enjoy 'being' other people — dressing up as mums and dads, old ladies, teachers, soldiers, tramps.

Character work such as that described here extends their experience of this. As they go into character work more deeply, their awareness of other people's individual personalities will increase and they will observe people's behaviour more carefully, leading to greater understanding.

Waxworks

This is a good introduction to character work for juniors, and it can be done with older children as well. Everyone finds a space. 'Who has been to Madame Tussaud's? There are lots of different waxworks there, kings, queens and famous people, all absolutely still.

'Now, in a moment, when I say the word 'Waxworks', you are all going to become waxworks, and the first kind of waxwork you are going to be is a teacher. So, without saying anything, let's see everyone starting to be a teacher, doing what a teacher does . . . and . . . Waxworks!' Everyone freezes in the position of a teacher, writing on the blackboard, ticking off a class, helping someone with their work. You can walk among the waxworks, commenting on the concentration and degree of realism. 'And now, in a minute, Susan's waxwork is going to come to life, so sit down, on the floor, the rest of you and . . . Action' and Susan's waxwork comes to life:

'Stop that talking at once! There's too much noise in this room . . .' and so on.

Then the children can make waxworks of other sorts: a mother or father (not necessarily their own mother or father), a person at work, a criminal, a clown, a monster, a crank . . . each time, one or more of the characters can be brought to life on 'Action' and go back to being a waxwork again on 'Freeze'.

One-line characters

This is another way into character work. Take a group of about six or seven children and ask them all to be a mum or a dad — and ask them for one phrase or sentence illustrating what that person would say and do (i.e. one line to establish the character). Then, still in the same characters, ask one of them to give one line which that person would say when angry; another to be happy; another sad, and so on.

Take another group of children and change the character to a teacher, or a doctor, a lorry driver, a salesgirl in a boutique, or a market stall-holder. There are many characters they can do; after starting with the more familiar mum and dad type characters, develop to less straightforward ones: tv compere, businessman, comedian, a crank, man in man's shop, football spectator, professional sportsman, politician, scientist, pop singer, film star, wife whose husband has left her/or vice versa, bus conductor, waitress, priest, etc., concentrating on believability rather than caricature.

One-line characters can be extended so that you hear more than one line of what the character says and does. If desired, 'Action' and 'Cut' can be used as a starting and stopping device.

A variation of this is to take a group of seven boys and girls and let each represent one of the seven deadly sins

(pride, sloth, envy, covetousness, lust, anger, gluttony).
Again, start with them as one-line characters, extending
further later on.

Characters and emotions, etc.

For this, slips of paper must be prepared; written on them
are adjectives describing emotions or other characteristics,
e.g. kind, cruel, aggressive, sensitive, inquisitive.

As in one-line characters, a group of six or seven
children are chosen, and each draws a slip from out of the
hat and has to be a character that could be described by
the word on the slip of paper. For example, if they have
drawn 'kind', they become a kind person. To start with
they work as in one-line characters, just giving one
sentence or phrase of what that person might do and say.
Later, you can extend it, through the use of 'Action'
and 'Cut', to longer pieces.

After a while, you can choose two suitably matched
characters from the group and give them about five
minutes to prepare a short duologue using those
characters in, say, a home setting, or at a table in a café,
or on a park bench, or you can give them a free choice.

Later on, another development is to divide the class
into pairs and let each person choose a slip of paper
with an adjective on it. Each pair has to prepare a
duologue on any theme they choose using characters
described by the words on the slips of paper.

More words that can be used are: proud, greedy, shy,
nervous, stupid, friendly, careless, clumsy, mad, old,
peculiar, bad-tempered, worried, angry, happy, conceited,
ignorant, sexy, overworked, depressed, enthusiastic,
intelligent, sad.

If you put the words on slips of paper, there is no
risk that anyone will feel that an adjective has been
assigned for personal reasons.

Characters from costumes

Ideas for characters can be suggested by clothes as well. If costume is available, juniors can be asked to dress up, which is always fun, and then improvise a character suggested by their costumes — the person who wears those clothes in real life. The work can be organized in the same way as 'one-line characters' and 'characters and emotions'.

With a more experienced group, you can allocate them items of clothing at random. Ask them to develop characters based on that costume and to prepare a piece of work, either working singly or in pairs, or as a group in a specified location, e.g. home, restaurant, bus stop, airport lounge.

General characters

We now come to the stage where the class are interested in developing characters of their own devising.

The character must be regarded as a three-dimensional, flesh and blood, real-life person — one must get to know what it feels like to be that person.

It is here that careful preparation and thought is necessary. Each person must research his character. What is his name? How old is he? Where does he live? The details are all important.

One way of organizing this work is to have a 'Character of the Week' spot, followed up by constructive comments from teacher and class.

The characters can be seen in monologue in various settings, e.g. giving their thoughts aloud on a park bench, in half-a-duologue (i.e. conversation with an imaginary other person), or they can be prepared in pairs, in order to work in duologue form. Costume can be used.

If necessary, you can offer them suggestions on which to build a character: a teacher or Head (always very popular); a clairvoyant; a barrow boy or old Woman from the market; a spoilt child; the Maestro; the vicar; a young child; Mad Harry; Oscar Goldwater, the Film Producer; a hypochondriac, a pop star; a small-time crook; a schizophrenic . . . .

Later, you can bring three or four of the established characters together in a specified location like a restaurant. or a doctor's waiting room.

People Meet People

This is a piece of work in which we can explore a character really deeply, with the whole class working together.

'People Meet People' is an imaginary television programme. There is a chairman, a guest and a studio audience. To start with, the chairman can be the teacher, the guest will be the character we are going to find out about, and the studio audience will be the members of the class. The idea of the programme is that a varied selection of people are invited to be guests week by week, and the studio audience can ask them any questions they like, about themselves, their life, and their opinions.

So a typical programme might begin with the chairman talking to an imaginary camera:

Ch: 'Good Afternoon, and welcome to People Meet People, the programme in which we get the chance to meet, and talk to, people from all walks of life. This week our studio audience is made up of children from the Mozart Road Secondary School, and our first guest is Mrs Lily Skinner, known to her friends as Lil, who has lived in the same district as the children live in for over eighty years. Lil, to start off the questions, may I ask just how old you are?'

Lil: 'Eighty-five last birthday, love.'

The first few questions come from the Chairman, then it is thrown open to the audience.

Q. (from the audience): 'Do you think the world's a
better place today than when you were a child?'

Lil: 'No, dear, I don't. We knew how to enjoy our-
selves in those days. People today with all their cars
and their colour tellies; they don't get no plaesure out of
it. Not like we used to.'

Q: 'Do you have any children and grandchildren?'

Lil: 'I've got three boys but one of them was killed
in the war. I've got grandchildren and great-grandchildren
now.'

Q: 'What do you like to have for breakfast in the
morning?'

And so it continues, for as long as you like. Each guest
is a character that someone has prepared.

In order for this to work there must be complete
belief in the situation from everybody, and it is necessary
for the audience to listen very carefully so that they can
follow up the answers to earlier questions.

Instead of using the format of a tv programme, the
same sort of thing can be done using the characters as
visitors to the school, and the class and teacher as themselves.

2 PROPS

The Telephone

A telephone is a most useful prop — an absolute must
for the basic equipment of a drama class. A battery-
operated electric bell (purchased from any hardware
store) is also needed.

Answering the phone

The telephone is placed on a box in the middle of the
room with a chair next to it. The teacher rings the bell
and beckons someone to answer the phone. They can

talk to the 'person' on the line about anything, but to
start with the teacher can brief them specifically
beforehand. For example, they can be told that when
answering the phone they will receive good news, or bad
news, or receive a surprise, or have a gossipy conversation.
After each call the teacher rings the bell and someone
else comes out to answer the phone.

Later on, the exercise can be for the person to say only
'yes' or 'no', or talk in gibberish . . . or the call can be
one that makes you happy, sad, angry, bored, afraid,
annoyed . . . or the call can be from someone you love, or
maybe from someone you love but they don't know it.

One must always be aware of the 'person' on the line.
It is important to *listen* to that 'person' as well as speak
to them.

This can be done with all ages.

Making a call

Each person in turn makes a call, remembering to be
accurate with details like the number of digits he dials.
Again, the class can make up their own personal calls or
you can give them a specific brief such as ringing up
someone to make a complaint, or to break off a boy-
girl relationship, or with a particular beginning like 'Is
Mr Johnson there?', or a given ending, or phoning the
police, the butcher, the doctor, the dentist, a friend, or
a repair man. If ringing one of these people, each caller
must be sure to give his name and address, unless it is a
person who would recognize him by his voice.

An effective piece of situation drama using the telephone is 'The Prowler in the Next Room.'

You tell the subject:

'You are on your own in the house and to your horror
you hear someone prowling in the next room. Very
gingerly, you make a telephone call for help to the police

or someone else. The prowler must not hear you.'
Perhaps he will accidentally knock over a lighter or
other prop, thus building up the suspense even more.

The Telephone Game

Ask the class to think of a word each, the first one that
comes into their heads. It could be Scheherezade, outside,
chicken, thimble, fingers, think, yellow. Ask each of them
to say the word they're thinking of; then ask some of
them to make a phone call bringing the word they have
chosen in to the conversation. Naturally, you will choose
the difficult words, and there must be complete concentration – no giggling.

Telephone conversation and dialects

Telephone conversations provide a handy and informal
way of doing work on dialects.

The telephone bell rings and members of the group
answer the telephone, in turn, each time having a conversation using a different accent or dialect.

As soon as one conversation ends, the bell rings again.
Once a dialect has been used once, it cannot be used
again. Go round the group until you run out of dialects.

Dialects and accents that can be used include: Posh
English, Cockney, Scottish, Welsh, Irish, Lancashire,
Yorkshire, Birmingham, West Country, American (several
kinds), West Indian, Indian, African, Australian, French,
German, Italian, Russian, Japanese.

The Frustrated Secretary

This is a fun piece of sketch drama in which you have a
secretary with three phones on her table. Phone A starts
ringing. She answers it. There is a Very Angry Person on
the line. She tries valiantly to pacify him. Phone B starts
to ring. She picks it up with her free hand, pleading with

the Very Angry Person to hold the line for one minute. Phone B is another Very Angry Person and desperately she tries her best with him. Then back to A again, who apparently is in a fury by now, and thus she goes back and forth from A to B working up a great frustration. The climax of this sketch drama is when phone C rings. The frustrated secretary lets out an almighty scream, or breaks down and sobs, or ends it in any way she chooses.

Crossed Lines

Three telephones are needed for this. If you don't have three, they can be mimed.

Anne rings Kim, telling her about the latest film on at the Odeon, her new bargain tights, her latest boy-friend, and other girlie gossip. Someone breaks into their conversation on a crossed line. Leave it to Kim and Anne to deal with him in whatever way they like. They could be very annoyed, insisting the intruder get off the line straightaway, or they could play it for fun. It's two against one — the intruder responds as best he can.

Pick a Bag

It's useful to have a box of bags in your basic equipment. A shopping bag, evening bag, satchel, brief-case, hand bag, shoulder bag, even a suitcase.

In the same way as in one-line characters, ask members of the class to pick a bag and take their character from the kind of bag it is. For example, if it's a shopping bag it could be a hard-working housewife for ever worried about rising prices; a brief-case might suggest a spruce business man from the City, and so on.

First see the characters individually, and then couple them in suitable pairs at a specified location, like at the bus stop.

Pick a Pair of Glasses

Like bags, spectacles are useful props for the basic equipment of a drama class. There are many kinds: swept up at the sides; black, square and studious; dark glasses; water goggles; rimless spectacles; National Health style; gold rimmed; tinted lenses.

'Pick a Pair of Glasses' is an idea carried out on the same lines as 'Pick a Bag', taking your character from the type of glasses, e.g. an unfashionable National Health pair might conjure up a weakling character, a natural butt for the school bullies. Some fashionable sunglasses might suggest a sexy lady sunning herself on a Costa Brava beach, surrounded by admirers.

After seeing each of the characters on their own, you can couple pairs of them in a convenient setting, such as sharing the same table in a crowded restaurant.

Pick a Prop

A member of the group selects a prop from the props table and improvises a situation centred round the prop. For example, the prop chosen could be a mirror. A girl might improvise a situation in which she critically contemplates her face. What can she do about those freckles? Why are her eyes not bigger? People say she's got a nice smile, though . . . .

Other 'Pick a Prop' monologue situations can be centred round a whistle, a violin, a football rattle, a string of beads, a doll (it can represent a baby), knitting, and many more.

The indefinite prop and the imaginary prop (see page 58) are linked with this piece of work.

The Seat

Seat Perching. A chair is placed in the middle of the room and children in turn find a new way of perching themselves on it: it could be kneeling on it, or doing a head stand on it, or sitting cross-legged, or they can turn the seat upside down and perch on it that way round. Once one way has been attempted the next person must find a new way. The teacher should stand in easy reach of the seat in case of minor tumbles.

If the class is small enough, another way that Seat Perching can be done is for everybody to find a place with their chairs and then to perch on it in their own ways and freeze; then for each of them to find a second position and freeze, and then a third. You can do the same thing, but without the seat, using the four basic levels: first lying, then sitting, then kneeling, then standing, and making the positions as dramatic and acrobatic as possible.

Seat Perching in Pairs can be done with two people to each seat.

The Different Kinds of Seat. A chair is placed in the middle of the room. The teacher says 'It's a burning hot seat' and picks a child who is to sit on it.

The child walks out from his place; it looks like a perfectly ordinary chair, and he is going to sit down on it, and . . . 'Yow!', he stumbles back to his place, rubbing his burnt behind.

This is an exercise in believability and the teacher can say whether he thinks the child's reaction is true or false: the child sustains his reaction from the burning hot seat all the way back to his own place.

Next, the seat can have an imaginary drawing pin on it, or wet paint, it can be a throne, a seat with glue on it, a slippery seat, a seat with itching powder on it, a smelly seat, one with a comfortable cushion, a seat next to someone you don't like, next to someone you love, a seat in a church, a seat with someone already sitting on it, and so on.

This is very popular with juniors but can be done by all ages if pitched at a suitable level.

Free Improvisation

The idea of this is for the teacher, using stage blocks
and whatever other equipment is to hand, to quickly
lay out a simple arrangement of them in the acting
area. Then, in ones or twos, members of the class have
to do an improvisation using this as their set.

As he is setting up, the teacher may say 'I want you
to look carefully at this set, and think to yourselves,
what can this represent? It can be anything you like;
indoors, outdoors, at home, at work. In a minute we're
going to see, first in ones and then in twos, what you
think might happen in this setting.'

The more interpretations that can be put on the set,
the better. Suppose you have laid out a bench, and a
stage block next to it with two open boxes on their
sides on top of this. Someone might see this as a park
with an abstract sculpture in it, with a boy meeting a
girl on the bench. Alternatively, the boxes could be
rabbit hutches, and a child could discover his rabbit
had run away, or they could be filing shelves in an
office, or a cupboard at home.

3 COSTUMES

Masks

Masks and Movement. When donning a mask, the body
must take on the character of the mask in a deliberate
way. For instance, if the mask is a sad clown, the body
becomes a droll, drooping, listless figure. If it's a devil's
mask, the body becomes spiky, dynamic and frightening.

Everyone dons a mask and examines his appearance in
a mirror. Divide the class into two halves. The first half
put on their masks and move round the room, expressing
their characters in a bold, uninhibited way. Music is
useful to set the mood for this. The other half watches.

Then they change over. Individuals who have developed the deliberate and dramatic movements can be picked out again for everyone to watch. This can be done with all ages.

Specific masked dance dramas can be set to suitable music. For example, '*The Happy Clown and the Sad Clown*'.

Enter the Sad Clown, all languid and droopy, shaking his head miserably — nobody laughs at his jokes. He is joined by the Happy Clown, with light, frisky movements, clapping his hands — everyone laughs at *his* jokes.

The Happy Clown spots the Sad Clown and good-naturedly capers across to him, shaking him warmly by the hand. The Sad Clown limply shakes his hand and mournfully shakes his head from side to side. The Happy Clown realizes that something is wrong and mimes 'What's up?'. The Sad Clown shakes his head again. Nobody laughs at his jokes. The Happy Clown puts an arm round the Sad Clown and, trying to cheer him up, tells him a few jokes (in mime), throwing his head back and laughing and slapping his new friend jovially on the shoulder. But, alas, to no avail; the Sad Clown continues to shake his head mournfully. The Happy Clown tries to teach the Sad Clown to do a mock bow: the Sad Clown tries but it is a pale imitation. Nothing works. In the end they part company, the Happy Clown capering back to the circus. The Sad Clown stands alone, utterly downcast.

Many masks can be worked into dance dramas, depending on what's in your stock. Carnival masks can be bought; otherwise they can be made out of papier mâché, and painted; flat masks can be made by cutting out colour photographs from magazines and mounting them on stiff paper, cutting out eye holes and attaching elastic or ribbons.

Mask characters

Someone selects a mask character — a space creature,
an old woman, a baby, a squirrel, Mickey Mouse — and
examines himself in the mirror, exploring the effect of
various mimes and movements. When wearing a full
mask, one's voice cannot be heard properly, so two
people work together; one wears the mask and the other
is his voice, staying at the side out of sight.

Suppose we have a space creature: he glides into view
and speaks in an unearthly monotone: 'I have arrived from
Planet 142 857. Planet Earth is to be investigated. I see
living creatures.' Moving all the time in a space-creature-
like way, he goes up to one of them, a fair-haired girl
wearing a blue dress. 'Here is one of them. It has yellow
fur on its head, and a blue skin on its body. It is a good
specimen. I shall take it on board the spaceship for our
zoo', and so it goes on.

It is important that the Mask and the Voice should
work together, the movements harmonizing with the
words as they improvise.

Mask characters can also be portrayed using two masks
and two voices working together, in pairings like the
baby and the ghost, Frankenstein and Blondie, two
piglets, the old woman and the devil, the beautiful lady
and the spy, etc., depending of course on your selection
of masks. It is interesting how such seemingly diverse
characters can fit together well.

Pick a Hat

It doesn't take long to build up a collection of hats of
different kinds — a policeman's helmet, a baby's bonnet,
a balaclava, a workman's cap, a chef's hat, a fez, a
bowler, a jockey's cap, a crown, a woolly cap, a trilby, a
flowered hat, a broad-brimmed summer hat, a sombrero,
a bathing cap, a beret . . ..

Take a group of about six and ask them all to pick a hat, look at it and put it on. They are going to become the person that wears that kind of hat, and we are going to see and hear a little of what that person might say and do. In other words, with one line they are going to establish the character of the person who would wear that hat. This can develop from hearing one line to hearing a lot more of each character. Then you can put two suitable characters together to work as a pair — they are to meet each other in the street, or whatever.

Pick a Hat can also be done by asking for a different dialect to fit each hat, or using different emotions — the angry hats, when everyone in the line of hats is angry, the proud hats, when each person takes on a proud character, and so on.

The same idea can be used with *wigs,* if you have them. Also, a slightly different variation is *scarves* (see page 77), or you could give them a choice: Pick a Hat, Wig or Scarf.

These ideas can be used with all ages, provided you pitch them at the right level.

Two Hats, Two Characters

This is a more advanced idea which demands quick thinking and concentration.

From the box of hats someone selects two with which he improvises a situation using the hats to represent two different people. For example, he might pick a cub scout's cap and a smart hat with a spray of cherries on it. When he is wearing the cub's cap he will be a cub scout and when he is wearing the smart hat with cherries on it he will be a Posh Lady. He dons the cub scout's cap and turns to the right to the imaginery Posh Lady, saying 'Excuse me, Miss, have you got any jobs that need doing?' He then quickly takes off the cub scout's cap

and puts on the smart hat with cherries on it, becoming
the Posh Lady, and turning left to the imaginary cub
scout, says 'Well, let me see, I suppose you could take the
dog for a walk.' Then quickly off with the smart hat
and on with the cub scout's cap: 'Do you mean the big
alsatian you've got chained up in the yard?' . . . etc.

It is important in Two Hats, Two Characters to use
two different voices for the two different characters and
to keep the eye level realistic, not talking to someone
as if they were either ten feet tall or two inches small.
Total concentration and belief in the situation are needed
to change from one character to the other quickly.

The same exercise can be done with wigs.

The Helmet that Won't Fasten

This is a piece of sketch material, done as a monologue,
about a crash helmet that won't fasten.

The boy has always been told by his mum that he must
wear a crash helmet when going out on his motor bike –
he knows it makes sense. The boy has to pick up his girl
friend at Waterloo Station at three o'clock. It is now
half past two. He lives half an hour away from the
station. He'll just about make it – except that he's not
going to be able to fasten his helmet. That is the brief
given to the boy.

He puts on his helmet – but the buckle won't do up.
He takes it off, examines the clasp. There doesn't seem
to be anything wrong with it. He puts it on again. Still
it won't tie. He tries several times, struggling with the
buckle. The thing simply will not fasten. He becomes
more desperate. Leave it to the boy to end it as he
pleases.

Scarves

From a collection of scarves (headscarves, neck scarves,

football scarves, chiffon scarves, saris, etc.) a group of
about six people pick one each. Each wears his scarf in
a different way — it could be worn simply as a headscarf,
as a hippie bandana, as a neckerchief, as a bandage nursing
a broken knee, as a sling, in charlady style, in pirate style,
like a belt, as a shawl — and, in the same manner as in
Pick a Hat, from the style he has chosen, he finds a
character to fit the way the scarf is worn, starting with
one line to establish the character and developing it later
on.

The Gloves that Have a Life of Their Own

Take a pair of gloves (they could be an old pair of
washing-up gloves or mittens, or boxing gloves) and
place them in the middle of the floor. 'These gloves are
magic gloves; when someone puts them on the magic
begins — the gloves have a life of their own; they take
over and control the movements of your hands.'

Someone comes out to put on the gloves. 'I'd better
start on the washing up', but as soon as he puts the
gloves on they take over, perhaps by pulling his arms
up into the air and down to the ground, twisting and
turning him round, making him punch at thin air,
sending him tumbling all over the floor, clutching towards
his neck to throttle him. Either he can escape from the
gloves' power by flinging them off, or else at the word
'Freeze' their magic wears off and he stops still.

This is a very popular idea. If you have a number of
pairs of gloves you can use that number of children all
wearing gloves at the same time. With older boys and
girls the magic needn't have the violent physical effect
you usually get with young ones. The effects can be more
subtle — it's up to their imagination.

The Shoes that Have a Life of Their Own works in
the same way as the gloves.

FIVE

Situation Drama and Improvised Plays

The situation drama ideas set out in this chapter are, on the whole, designed to be carried out by a small group of two to four children, on their own, directed by the teacher, and without preparation. These ideas are suitable for children with some experience in basic drama, who show a readiness to move on.

In nearly all the ideas there is a strong element of conflict, and this is vital for dramatic purposes; from the educational point of view, this helps children learn to understand and deal with conflict situations.

In situation drama, the smaller the group the easier it is to work with: when starting off, a pair of children is ideal. This is because, for satisfactory drama, each member of the group must be aware of all the others. With five or six inexperienced children, this is rather too demanding, and the result tends to be confusing and chaotic. Also, look at real life. What size are the groups that form in the street, at home, in the school playground? How many people can sit round a meal table before two separate conversations develop?

The direction given before a piece of work in improvised situation drama is all important. State who the characters involved are, and give a brief description of the situation, seen from the characters' point of view. To stimulate the children's imagination, you can list some of the possible ways the scene may develop. A lot depends on how experienced the children are. The less experienced they are, the more guidance they will need,

but whatever stage they are at, the brief you give them
must be clear and positive.

Comments and criticisms afterwards are very important; they will improve the work, as well as developing
the children's critical faculties. Invite the rest of the
class to comment, always encouraging constructive
comments rather than destructive ones. Find out what
members of the group liked about the piece and why
they liked it. Encourage children to praise each other;
this fosters a friendly atmosphere in the class so that
people will become less inhibited in what they do in
front of the others. Make your own comments; it is best
to be concise and limit yourself to the two or three most
important points. Try to give praise if you can. Criticism
can be depersonalized by referring to a general point of
technique: 'Most of us couldn't see Tilly's face when she
was opening the parcel, because Michael was masking her.
So remember, when you're working with an audience,
don't mask each other.' In this way, points of stage
technique can be brought in as and when the work
demands it.

A question that is often asked is 'Should the teacher
intervene if a piece of work in improvisation seems to
be going on too long and getting nowhere?' Clearly, this
is a matter for individual judgement as to whether the
work will benefit from your intervention; 'Try to find an
ending' or 'Twenty seconds to finish' will usually serve to
bring about a satisfactory conclusion without anyone
feeling that they have been stopped in full flight.

Some teachers prefer to do situation drama by
dividing the whole class up into groups of three, or whatever, and having them all do their improvisations at the
same time, the idea being that the children will work
more uninhibitedly with fewer people watching them,
and also to use time more efficiently by having more

children work at the same time. The drawbacks of this
method are that it tends to produce a high noise level,
which reduces concentration, and there is little opportunity for the invaluable comments and feedback from
the teacher and the rest of the class.

Here is a selection of situation drama ideas for two or
more people, most of them written as they might be
introduced to a class by the teacher.

1 PLOTS

The Borrowed Dress

'Kay and Angela are two sisters. Kay, you have borrowed
Angela's dress without asking her permission and,
Angela, you go to the wardrobe because you want to
wear this dress tonight for a party, and you find it with
a horrible stain down the front. You realize that Kay
must have borrowed it without telling you, and you are
absolutely furious. It's six o'clock and you're going out
at half past six. There's no time to take it to the dry
cleaners or do anything that will clean it up. So you take
the dress and storm in to Kay with it, and there's Kay
coolly filing her nails on an emery board, and you really
have it out with her . . . you can end it in whatever way
you like.'

The Burnt Trousers is a corresponding idea for two
boys. This time, one brother's new pair of trousers have
been borrowed by the other, and they have been burned.

The Babysitter

'Sue, you are a young mother with a beautiful baby girl,
Tracy. Phil, you are the boy next door and can earn
fifty pence for yourself by babysitting for Sue. One
Saturday evening, while you are babysitting for her, the
phone rings and Terry, who lives across the road, invites
you over to listen to his new stereo. It'll only be for

a minute, the baby'll be all right, you reckon. You go
over to Terry's place. The scene starts when Sue returns
to the house. Sue enters calling "Phil, I'm back! Phil!
Phil?" It soon dawns on you, Sue, that Phil has left the
baby by herself! You pick Tracy up in your arms, very
worried, but she's all right. Your anger with Phil starts
to grow and then he returns . . . and you can take it on
from there. So we start with Sue coming in, expecting to
find Phil and Tracy together . . . .'

The Lost Five-pound Note

'I want a mum and her son. Susan Onigbanjo, will you
be the mum? And John Williams, will you be Susan's son?
Now, John, you're a very good boy who does all the
shopping for your mum every week. This Friday, as usual,
you go to the supermarket and get all the shopping for
the week – baked beans, tomato soup, bread, biscuits,
washing powder, etc. – but when you come to pay for
it with the five-pound note mum's given you, the money
has gone, it is not in your pocket. We start off with John
coming home to mum *without* the shopping. And mum
says something like "Hello, John! Where's the shopping,
then?" John breaks the news. Take it on from there and en
it in any way you like.'

The Lost Gem Stone

'Martha and Vicky, you are two sisters and you get on
very well together, share each other's clothes and all that
kind of thing. Vicky, you lend your lovely pearl ring to
Martha for the Valentine's Disco. Martha, you had a
lovely time and danced all night with Steve. It was a
fabulous evening. You came home very happy. You looked
at the ring. The pearl had gone! It must have fallen out
when you were dancing with Steve. So we start when
Martha approaches Vicky and has to explain what's

happened. Vicky, you might react angrily or you might
be sympathetic.'

The Lost Football

'Let's have two brothers, Steve and Graham Fletcher.
You are both football fanatics. Graham, you have
borrowed Steve's football to play in the street; but
you were robbed of it by the Maxwell Street mob: it
was six against one; you didn't have a chance. We start
with Graham entering and explaining to Steve what
happened. Steve, you react as you think you would.
You might be mad at Graham, you might be sympathetic — it's up to you . . . .'

The Dyed Red Hair

'Pauline, you're a young housewife who has been feeling
very restless lately. You need a change! They say a change
is as good as a rest. You decide to dye your mousy hair
red. Now, let's see you sitting in front of the telly with
your new red look, wondering what your husband, John,
will say when he comes home. We start when John comes
in from work, and reacts as he feels . . . .'

The Pet that Died

'Bernadette, I want you to be Dexter's mum. Dexter,
you play your own age. Dexter comes back from school
at four-fifteen and today mum has some very sad news
for him — his lovely black dog, Samson, has been run over
by a car early this afternoon and is . . . dead. Mum has
to tell Dexter. She knows it will break his heart because
Dexter loved that dog. The first thing Dexter always
does when he comes home from school is to call "Samson! Samson!" and the two of them play together. Now,
Dexter, today you come in as usual at four-fifteen and

say "Hello Mum! Samson! Samson! Where are you,
Samson?" . . . So let's take it from there.'

Latch Key Kids

'I want a brother and a sister — let's have a real-life
brother and sister: Frankie and Gloria Leon. Let's say
that your mum works till seven o'clock in the evening,
so there is no one at home to let you in after school —
therefore, Frankie, being the elder of the two, is in
charge of the key, which he always wears on a string
round his neck. Now, on this particular day you both
hurry home from school and you're very anxious to get
indoors as quickly as possible as your favourite science-
fiction tv programme starts immediately after school.
You arrive, panting, at the doorstep — and, Frankie,
you go to take the key from round your neck — but the
key is missing — it is not there. What happens then
between the pair of you is, of course, up to you. Are you
going to miss your favourite programme? Are you going
to be locked out till your mum comes home? Can you
get in through a window? Has the key dropped off some-
where between school and home? Let's take it from when
you arrive at the doorstep, out of breath, having run all
the way from school.'

RSPCA

'Chris, you are walking home from school, whistling away
to yourself, when you see a man brutally kicking a dog.
You are shocked and immediately call out to him to stop.
The man doesn't stop and, Chris, you know you must do
something. You'd call the police and report the man to
the RSPCA — but there are no policemen around. You
try and persuade the man to stop. Callum, will you be the
man and, Dexter, will you be the poor unfortunate dog?
Can you whine, Dexter? Right! So let's see, first of all,

the man getting angry with the dog, and then, after a few moments, along will come Chris . . . .'

You can have an imaginary dog, instead of having a child representing it.

Two Girls, Same Boyfriend

'Nula and Linda, you are sisters. We start off with Nula on the phone to her boyfriend, Mario. Mario, you are not seen or heard at this stage. While Nula is murmuring sweet nothings to Mario, Linda comes in, pauses, and stands at the back of the room, listening in on the conversation. You hear the name Mario being mentioned several times in a rather tender way. And Mario is not a very common name. When Nula puts the phone down, Linda has it out with her. It transpires that you have the same boyfriend — Mario has been two-timing the pair of you. And so you sisters have a good old sisterly row. The scene reaches a climax when Mario arrives, brandishing a new girl on his arm (that is you, Sandra) and asks if the two sisters would like to go bowling and make up a foursome.

So we start with Nula on the phone . . . .'

Wrong Change

'I want a busy, no-nonsense mum. You, Taiwo, Mrs Ajenusi! Let's say you've got five kids, that is five mouths to feed plus, of course, a hungry, hard-working husband, and yourself. So when you do the shopping you've got to count the pennies very carefully; it's very difficult to make ends meet. Now, on this particular day you've just popped out to the supermarket to buy some washing powder, some baked beans and two packets of fish fingers. You pay the girl on the till (Joanne, will you be the girl on the till?) a five-pound note and the girl gives you the change, but it's only the change from a pound. Mrs Ajenusi, you look at the change, saying something like "Hey, I gave you a five-pound note and you've only given me the change for a pound". Joanne, you deny this. You are sure it was one pound that Mrs Ajenusi gave you. Now maybe she's made a mistake, or maybe she's trying to cheat Mrs Ajenusi. And what an argument the two of you have. End it in whatever way you like.'

The Motorists

'Phil and Terry, you are two motorists. Can you each use a red, oblong stage block to represent your car? You are driving along when the cars crash. Terry runs into the back of Phil. Both drivers get out to inspect the damage. Phil accuses Terry of being the guilty party and vice versa. End it as you please.'

The Saleslady and the Customer

'Katherine, you are a very persuasive saleslady. You get a commission on every garment you can sell – and the commission soon adds up to a very tidy sum; without it, your wages are very low. Jenny is a customer who is looking for a dress, but is not quite sure what she wants. Jenny comes in to Katherine's shop, and Katherine has to try and sell something to her, being as persuasive as possible. It's up to you both whether a purchase is made or not.'

This situation can be adapted to a saleslady or salesman in any kind of shop.

The Malingerer

'Hayley, you are a sensible and conscientious mum. Your son is, you, Tommy Pender! Tommy, Hayley is your mum and you, I'm afraid, are a bit of a trickster and this particular morning you don't feel like going to school so

you try to persuade Mum that you're not well — though
there is nothing whatsoever the matter with you. You
start by saying you have a slight headache — but that
doesn't seem to wash with Mum. Your headache gets
worse, you feel really sick! You make a great show of the
agony you are suffering! Perhaps Mum then suggests
calling the Doctor? I'll leave it to you to see how it ends.
Maybe Hayley sees through Tommy and packs him off to
school — maybe Tommy puts on a convincing case and
gets away with a day off school!'

Argument Over TV Channels

'Beverley and Clovis, you are brother and sister and the
pair of you are telly addicts. Now, Beverley's favourite
programme is Top of the Pops while Clovis always wants
to watch football. On this particular evening, Top of the
Pops and Football Special coincide on opposite channels.
Beverley stubbornly insists on watching Top of the Pops.
Clovis argues back with equal fervour for Football
Special. You fight it out between you! But fight with
words, not fists! Let's see who wins!'

The Crook and the Girl in the Jewellers'

'Maggie, you work in a very expensive jewellers' in the
West End of London. Now, normally you are not alone
in the shop but on this particular day the other girl is
off sick and the manager has just been called away by a
phone call. It is eleven o'clock and you are not at all
busy, in fact the shop is empty, when a young man —
Shefki — enters carrying a small, black brief-case. The
young man is a crook, although Maggie does not yet
know this. The young man asks the girl if he can see
'Tray F' from the window display. Maggie goes and gets
Tray F but when she turns round Shefki has locked the
door, pulled the blind, and is pointing a small automatic

towards her. He tells her to give him the keys to the safe.
But, bravely, Maggie refuses. Shefki threatens her and
what happens then is completely up to you.

Trying to Borrow Money from a Stranger

'They say the quickest way to lose a friend is to lend
him money. Do you agree?'
   'Kiaran, you are at the bus stop when you discover, to
your horror, that you've lost your purse. You search your
bag frantically but your purse has definitely gone. Now
you are in a predicament because here you are in London
— it's four o'clock — and you've got to get all the way
to Reading by early evening. You need at least a couple
of pounds for fares. Also waiting at the bus stop is a
middle-aged lady. You explain to her what has happened
and ask if you can borrow two pounds from her. Elizabeth
will you be the lady and I'll leave it to you to decide
whether you believe Kiaran or not and whether you'll
lend her — or give her — the money.'

Many Years Ago . . .

'Let's have two old people sitting on a park bench —
Martin Phillips and Beverley Martin. You are both over
seventy years of age. You sit there reading your news-
papers and gradually engage each other in conversation.
Something one of you says makes you gradually realize
that you knew one another over fifty years ago. Suddenly
you recognize one another. This delights the pair of you
and you take a nostalgic trip down memory lane. You
reminisce about the people you once knew and what
became of them, the places you knew, the fashions, the
manners, the two world wars, the Royal Family, you
talk about young people today — whatever. End it as
you please.'

You can either specify that the old people are living today and looking back fifty years in the past, or that they are people of their own generation seen fifty years in the future.

Pride Goes Before a Fall

'There are some parents who believe that their child is God's gift to the world and find it very hard to take any adverse criticism whatsoever about their beloved offspring. Such a parent is you, Angela — let's call you Mrs Scott. Your daughter, Rachel, is an absolute menace in her class and everyone knows it except you, Mrs Scott. You are the last to know. Rachel's teacher, Miss Burdis (all right, Bernadette?) calls to see you to have a talk and, in the most tactful way possible, to give you the full facts about your daughter, Rachel — her bad behaviour, her mean and spiteful acts towards the other children, how spoilt and selfish she is — but Mrs Scott cannot believe her ears at what Miss Burdis has to say. As far as she, Mrs Scott, is concerned, the sun shines out of Rachel's very eyes. But Miss Burdis goes on to give a blow by blow account of Rachel's antics. She's very worried about it; it's disrupting the entire class. Rachel then returns from her friend's house and sees her mother and teacher both looking very uncomfortable. End how you like. Who would like to be Rachel? All right, you Kim Doyle. So Angela is Kim's mum, and Kim is Angela's spoilt little girl. Let's start with Miss Burdis ringing on the doorbell.'

The Broken Glasses

'Let's have two friends — Michael Murphy and Paul Parsons. One of you is wearing a new pair of glasses, so can Paul go and get a pair of glasses from the props box. Both of you boys are watching television and Michael asks Paul if he can try on his new glasses. Paul reluctantly agrees. You don't like letting other people put on your glasses, especially as they're a new pair. Michael tries them on and fools around in them and suddenly he drops them on the floor, and they break! Paul is horrified — and terrified of what his mum will say because these new glasses cost a few pounds and she'll go mad that they're broken on the very first day! Paul, you are really broken-hearted and scared about Mum, and furious with Michael. Michael, you are very sorry — but there's no good in just being sorry in this world. What can you do? Let's take it from the beginning — both boys are watching telly and Michael asks Paul if he can try on his new glasses.'

To Leave School or Not to Leave School

'Phil, you are sixteen years of age and are suffering from an attack of schoolitis. Academically, you are very bright and Mum wants you to stay on at school another two years to do your A-levels. You want to leave now, get a job and earn some money. We see both sides of the coin: you feel you've outgrown school and you're impatient to get started in the world outside as soon as possible, while from your mum's point of view — she wants her son to get those qualifications in order to get a better job later on. She can't see why you should want to leave. I want a good, strong, articulate mum-character: you, Kate Saunders, you be Phil's mum.

'So we start when Phil comes in from school, and tells his mum he's fed up with the place and wants to leave.'

The New Girl in the Office

'You are experiencing new things for the first time quite a lot in your lives. For instance, one of you may have eaten a new kind of food for the first time recently. Or

you may have started a new job for the first time. It can
feel a little strange but it can also be tremendously
exciting. Penny, you are the new girl in the office. You've
just started the job this very morning and you are feeling
keyed-up and full of anticipation. John is your Boss —
he is tall, dark, handsome, and quite young — and
married. You are sitting at your desk typing away when
the Boss enters the room and gives you some important
invoices that must be done urgently. He notices how very
attractive you are and asks you how you're getting on
with the new job, leading to a more personal conversation. You, Penny, are quite relieved to find that your
Boss is friendly and human, and flattered by his attention.
But in the next few minutes he is asking you out to
dinner. Well, how do you cope with that, Penny? He's
a married man. Let's take it from where we see Penny
typing efficiently and John, the Boss, enters with the
invoices.'

Six Months Apart

'Trevor and Tina, you are standing at the bus stop — but
you don't see one another — you, Trevor, are looking
one way and you, Tina, are facing the other way. In due
course you turn round and recognize each other straight
away. You are meeting quite by accident; you haven't
seen one another for six months. Now, what happened
six months ago is up to you. You may have been boyfriend and girlfriend and had a row, one of you might
have gone away on a long holiday or had an accident
and been in hospital . . . . Here we see you both after the
six-month interval — and what happens next?'

The Boss and the Employee

'Peter, you are the Boss. Let's say you are manager of the
Princess Chocolate Factory. Phil, you are one of Mr Daly's

employees. Peter, this is your office, carpet on the floor, three telephones — you're a bit of a big fish in a small pond. You send for Phil: maybe you are going to give him the sack; maybe you're going to promote him; maybe you have a complaint — or a compliment — Phil doesn't know — it's up to the Boss! We start with Phil knocking on the door, not sure what to expect.'

Smoking (1)

'Martin Kemp, you are sitting alone in the cloakroom; you have slipped out of Mr Webb's Maths class, and here we find you having a quick smoke. You are nervously puffing the cigarette, when suddenly Mr Webb enters! Terry Bush, will you be Mr Webb? And obviously, Terry, you are not pleased to see Martin in this situation. Smoking is against the rules.'

Smoking (2)

'Jenny, you are at home watching telly and you decide to have a secret smoke. Your mum's left her cigarettes lying on the table and you take one of them. Nobody'll know, you're alone in the house, or so you think. You've just settled down to a cigarette when to your dismay your mum returns (bingo ended early because of a power failure). Mum (will you be the mum, Maria?) is astonished to see her daughter smoking for the very first time. You are surprised and angry and upset. Maybe when you calm down you can offer your daughter some constructive advice. So we start with Jenny sitting watching telly . . . let's see you.'

Smoking (3)

'Kate, you are a chain-smoker complete with a smoker's cough. You tried to kick the habit several times but have never managed to give them up. You know it's ruining your health. You known all about cancer risks, how it diminishes your life span, makes you unfit, etc. So be it. You carry on smoking. Sally, you are Kate's daughter and you love your mother very much. You see what smoking is doing to her and you're very worried about the consequences. We see you both in the living room, Kate having a last cigarette before going to bed: Sally decides to have a heart to heart chat with Mum — you desperately want her to stop . . . before it's too late.'

The Parting

'Gillian, you are a widow. Let's say your husband died of heart trouble two years ago. He has left you with a too-boisterous son who you cannot control — nor can his school teachers do anything with him. Perry, will you be the son who nobody can do anything with? You're always getting into trouble at school and you get fed up being stuck at home with Mum.

Gillian, as a last resort, you have decided to send Perry to boarding school. Let's see your last few minutes together before the taxi comes to take Perry to the station. It is the very first time mother and son will have been parted. When the taxi man knocks at the door Perry will have to go, and that'll be the end of the scene.

Another Kind of Parting

'John Blundell, you are a soldier, very happily in love with and engaged to Caroline North. All was bliss until this morning when you received orders posting you overseas immediately. You are to be stationed in Northern Ireland for six months, which seems an eternity to you young lovers. We see the pair of you at Euston Station five minutes before the train leaves . . . .'

Popping the Question

'There comes a time in almost every young man's life when he finds a girl he loves and he asks her to marry him. Now, choosing the right time and place for this is very important; after all, you're asking the girl to spend the rest of her life with you.

Terry Bush, you've been going out with Kim Taylforth for nine months now and the time has come, you feel, to name the day, to propose — to pop the question. Here you both are in Clissold Park, Islington. It is a lovely Spring day. The time is right and so is the place Kim, I shall leave it to you as to whether you accept or reject. So, without in any way sending it up, you're sitting in the park, talking to one another, and Terry starts getting round to the subject . . . .'

Break-Up of a Marriage

'Paul and Veronique, you have been married for seven years and you, Veronique, want a divorce. It's not simply the seven-year itch but something rather more serious — you are expecting another man's child. That man lives next door; Ray Burdis, will you be the other man? You and Veronique are very much in love, and have been for the past year. Paul does not suspect.'

Ray: 'What about my wife, then?'

'Let's say you're unmarried. We start off with Paul and Veronique watching television and, Veronique, you broach the subject of your pregnancy with caution. Paul, not surprisingly, may take it very badly. An argument develops. And in the middle of it Ray comes in through the back door . . . .'

Prejudice

'Linda: you're going out with Elvis. Linda is white and Elvis is black. After they've kissed goodnight at the doorstep, Linda comes inside and sees Mum (you, Caroline) looking very displeased. Caroline, you object to Linda going out with Elvis just because he is black, because you are colour-prejudiced. Mother and daughter confront one another and an argument blazes up. First let's see it this way round. And then from the other way round with Elvis going home to Dad (you, Herbert), and Dad starts on Elvis about Linda — because she is white.'

The Facts of Life

'Bridget: you're a mum and your little girl — May — is no longer a little girl but is fast growing up. You've heard that there will be Sex Education lessons at school next term but you decide to teach your daughter the facts of life yourself. The two of you are sitting cosily together in the living room, Mum knitting and May reading a comic, and the time is right to tackle the subject . . . .'

This can also be done with father and son, mother and son, and father and daughter.

Mum and Mum-to-Be

'Sonia, let's say that you have a three-month-old baby girl. Fern is your friend who lives in the flat next door, and she is going to have a baby herself quite soon. Fern drops in for a cup of coffee, and after a while conversation turns to what it is like looking after a small baby. Let's start with Fern ringing on the doorbell . . . .'

Hitch-hike

'Kim, I want you to be a hitch-hiker. We see you on the A23, hitching from London to Brighton. Now, you know how potentially dangerous it is to hitch a lift on your own. But, I'm afraid to say, you are heedless of your parents' and teachers' advice and warnings. So, here you are, hitch-hiking from London to Brighton. An articulated lorry approaches — Ozzie, would you quickly assemble the Cab of the lorry using the red stage blocks, please, and Gary, will you be the lorry driver who picks up the hitch-hiker. I'll leave it to you to see what happens, if anything — you might have an argument; there might be an accident; the lorry driver might try and get fresh with her; or you might just have a pleasant conversation — it's up to you.'

Something Only Your Best Friend Can Tell You

'Kim and Alison, you are best friends. Kim, although you like Alison very much, there is just one thing that you do *not* like about her . . . maybe it's something personal like Alison suffering from BO . . . maybe Alison is very bitchy towards other people . . . maybe she steals. Whatever it may be is up to you, Kim, but one day, when you are sitting together, you decide it's time that you told Alison the truth about herself. Alison, you react in whatever way you like: you might be furious or humble, or you might retaliate by telling Kim a home-truth too.'

Telling Your Problems to a Stranger

'You've heard the proverb "A trouble shared is a trouble halved"? Well, have you ever been in a situation where you had a problem that you couldn't share, even with your most sympathetic friend — yet you would feel more at ease talking it through with a stranger?'

'Stephanie, you are on a train journey. You've got a problem: it can be a boy friend problem, a domestic problem, a problem at school or at work, whatever you like. You haven't been able to discuss it with anyone. There is someone with a sympathetic face sitting opposite you in the compartment. Sometimes it's easier to talk to a stranger than to a friend. You tell your problem to the stranger. Dawn, you are the stranger . . . .'

Bus Stop (1)

'There are two gossips at the bus stop: let's have Denise
Cook and Hayley Glassberg. You've been waiting for
half an hour for that 73 bus! So you're not exactly in
the best of moods — far from it. We hear you moaning
away to each other about the terrible bus service and
especially about how infrequent the 73 bus is. At last,
in the distance, Denise spots it coming. At last! The 73
bus arrives and you're both just about to climb on when
an inspector appears and orders the bus back to the
garage. Well, that's the last straw. The pair of you are
fuming. You've been waiting half an hour and after
all that, when the bus finally does arrive, it's sent back
to the garage! It's a disgrace! So the pair of you turn on
the bus inspector and put the blame on him. The
inspector — that's you, Chris Leonard — has got to stand
up for himself and do his best to explain the delay —
there's a shortage of staff, and the buses get held up in
traffic jams, and so on . . . and good luck to you, Chris,
with these two very angry ladies. So we start with the
two of you waiting at the bus stop.'

Bus Stop (2)

'Two women standing side by side at the bus stop — you,
Marijke, and you, Kay. You don't know one another.
You have been some time at the bus stop — waiting for
the 38 bus. At last it arrives. The bus conductor (Tommy,
the bus conductor, please) calls out "One, and one only!"
Marijke goes to climb on the bus and Kay immediately
says something like "Here! I was here first" and pushes
her way on in front of Marijke. Marijke objects, insisting
she was first in the queue. You argue it out between you
but in the end the bus conductor gets fed up with the
pair of you, rings the bell, and off goes the bus. Then

you've both missed the boat . . . or rather the bus! End it how you like.'

The Man from the Council

'Let's have a family, let's call it the Adams family. Peter, you be Dad, Gillian is Mum, and let's have Callum and Naomi as two of their four children. The other two are playing outside. You are all living in a three-roomed flat in very uncomfortable and overcrowded conditions. The heating system is inadequate and there is a lot of damp throughout the flat which you can't seem to get rid of. You've been on the Housing List for six years now and are forever hoping you will get one of these new flats the Council are building on the Elgar Estate. On this particular evening there is a knock at the door and it is the Man from the Council — Mr Williams (Herbert, will you be the Man from the Council?). Mr Adams invites Mr Williams in and Mr Williams takes out the housing application forms and discusses the situation with the family. Now, Mr Williams may be sympathetic, or maybe he is non-committal, or maybe he is totally pessimistic. What chance have the Adams family of getting one of those new flats on the Elgar Estate? Are they destined to stay where they are? They've got to try and persuade Mr Williams to help them. So let's start with the family at home, and after a few moments there comes a knock at the door . . . .'

Teacher Investigating Classroom Row

'Now, for this piece of work I am going to play the part of a teacher — not myself, but a different teacher, let's call her Mrs Selkirk — and all of you are going to be a class. I'm going to pounce on two of you as being the ringleaders in a row that took place in the classroom; you both react as if it was a real classroom row . . . then anyone who knows anything further, if they feel they can contribute to the investigation, can put up their hand, just as they would in real life.

'Lesley Theobald and Carol Byrne, come up to my desk at once! Now, I want the truth, the absolute truth . . . do either of you girls know anything about May Leon crying and running out of school after break?'

'No, Miss,' murmur Lesley and Carol.

'We're all going to stay here until we find out what did happen, so are you quite sure you don't know anything about it?'

'I don't know nothing, Miss,' says Carol.

'Lesley?'

'May stole my purse, Miss.'

'What makes you say that, Lesley?'

'It was gone, Miss, when I went to the cloakroom at break.'

'And what makes you accuse May Leon of stealing it? Did you see her take it?'

'No, Miss! But she had twenty pence in her hand at break and she had no money on her way to school this morning.'

Jennifer Brassett's hand goes up: 'Please, Miss, I know something about it.'

'Yes, Jennifer?' . . .

The investigation continues and more people can be brought in, with the entire class improvising together. Later, the teacher character can be played by one of the children.

2 PLAYLETS

Here is a simple format for improvised playlets, in which the director describes the characterization, basic plot, and structure of the playlet which is then enacted straightaway.

The playlets consist of three or four short acts divided by incidental music. The music begins and is faded out while the title is announced; then the playlet begins; music is faded in and out between each act. After the last act the participants come to the front and one after another, in character, give their thoughts aloud about the situation, as in a vox pop (see p. 128). Music again at the end.

Some examples of playlets
(i) The Dog that Must be Put Down
There are three characters: Mum, Dad and Child. There is an imaginary dog. The action takes place in their living room.
    Act One. Mum and Child. Mum tells the child that the dog is ill; it must be put down because it is suffering. The child is upset.
    Act Two. Child and Imaginary Dog. The child says goodbye to the dog.
    Act Three. Dad and Child at bedtime. Dad tries to cheer the child up. The child goes to bed, still unhappy.
    Act Four. Mum and Dad. They discuss how the child has taken the dog being put down and the effect it will have on him, and what they will do about it.
    Vox Pop. The thoughts aloud of the three characters.

(ii) The Bad School Report
There are four characters: Teacher, Mum, Dad and Child. The action takes place in the living room.
    Act One. Teacher and Mum. Teacher calls on Mum with the child's School Report. It is a very bad report. Teacher discusses it with Mum. Mum is very disturbed; she goes to get Dad. Teacher stays.
    Act Two. Teacher and Child. Child arrives home and is aghast to see the teacher there. Teacher is grim-faced and they talk about the bad school report.

Act Three. Later. Dad and Child. Dad enters in a furious temper. He has it out with the child about his bad work and behaviour. Child is sent to do his homework.

Act Four. Mum and Dad. They discuss their child's bad school report. Why has it happened?

Vox Pop. The thoughts aloud of the four characters.

Pitched at the right level, this can be done with either Junior or Secondary age-groups.

(iii) The Divorce

There are three characters: Mum, Dad and Child. The action takes place in the living room.

Act One. Mother and Child. Mum explains to Child that she and Dad haven't been getting on very well lately. In short, they are going to have a divorce. The child reacts strongly. What's going to happen to them all? Mum exits to kitchen to make tea.

Act Two. Dad and Child. Dad comes in to find the child crying and comforts him. He tries to explain the situation as best he can. Child is still very upset and goes out.

Act Three. Mum and Dad. Yet another row. This time they bring into the argument the effect of the divorce on the child.

Vox Pop. The thoughts aloud of the three characters.

3 LOCATIONS

Instead of giving the children an outline of a plot to trigger off a piece of work in situation drama, you can instead specify a location to provide the guidelines for the piece. For example:

The Lift

Draw a chalked rectangle (about six feet by four feet)

on the ground to represent the lift. Two or three children enter the lift together. Their destination is the top floor of the block of flats. One presses the button and the lift starts — but suddenly, on a given signal, the lift gets stuck. Let the situation develop naturally; after a while you can make another signal (shaking a rattle or ringing a bell) which means that the lift has started again — and will bring them back to safety once more.

Outside the Headmaster's Office

'Hussein, you are sitting outside the Headmaster's Office, waiting to see him. Maybe you've been sent to him for bad behaviour, maybe it's about your work, maybe he's going to congratulate you for something, maybe you don't know why you're there. Anyway, you're sitting there when along comes Raymond, who's also been sent to the Headmaster. Let's see what happens outside the Headmaster's office. End it in whatever way you like.'

Other suitable locations

In the back row at school.
At an adventure playground.
The Doctor's or Dentist's waiting room.
At the tube station.
In the Customs. (Customs Officer and Traveller attempting to smuggle watches.)
At the police station. (Desk Sergeant, Detective, Man 'helping police with their inquiries'.)
In the hairdressing salon.
The prison cell. (Possibly planning their next job?)
In a convent.
In bed. (The last two minutes before falling asleep.)
Another planet. (The spacemen clamber down from their spaceship on to the surface of a newly dis-

covered planet and meet intelligent creatures living
on it, for the first time.)
Outside your home, cleaning the car. (Two neighbours.)
The transport cafe. (Proprietor, Lorry Driver, Hell's
Angels.)
The jewellers'. (An engaged couple.)
In Heaven.
At the magistrate's court.

4 OTHER SITUATION DRAMA IDEAS
Excuses

'Charles, will you be the teacher and sit up at the top
of the room with your table and chair? You start giving
the class a lesson on matrices or French verbs or the
Russian Revolution, or whatever you like. Beverley,
you are late for school and you gingerly come into the
class and, perhaps, try and quietly make for your seat,
hoping not to be seen. But the teacher sees you and
demands a reason for your lateness. Beverley, you make
up an excuse. The teacher listens to Beverley's excuse
and deals with it as he thinks he should.'

'After Beverley we'll have others, each coming in, in
turn, and giving a different excuse for being late. Be
original if you can, but always be credible. You're a bit
scared of this teacher, and you want him to believe you,
so don't make the excuses too fantastic. Start off,
Charles, please, and let's have Beverley in position ready
to come in and give the first excuse.'

Gossips

'Let's have a shop. And there is a shopkeeper (you,
Sharon) and a customer (Pauline). Every Friday you
both have a good old gossip over the counter when
Pauline comes in to do her week-end shopping. This
particular Friday is no exception: you both have a fine

gossip about the neighbours, the cost of living, the milk-
man, the telly, the kids — you name it! It's up to you.'
    This gossip idea can be done in a variety of ways:
    Two housewives gossiping over a cuppa.
    Two schoolgirl gossips.
    Two people working on a factory assembly line.

The Pick-Up
'Theresa, you are on your own, at Highbury and Islington
underground station, one night. There is not a soul other
than yourself on the platform. Along comes Shefki. He
gives you the once over, reckons on you . . . decides he
definitely fancies you. Shefki, you try to pick up
Theresa. Now, Theresa, you've been told by your mum
a hundred times if you've been told once — never talk to
strangers. But maybe Shefki can produce a line of chat
that makes him irresistible. Let's see, Shefki, if you
succeed in picking up the lovely Theresa.
    'The pick-up can also take place at the bus stop or at
the cinema or at a dance. Roles can be reversed with the
girl picking up the boy.'

Letting Someone into your Confidence
'Anita, you and Lucy are friends and one of the lovely
things about friendship is the sharing of all sorts of
things: fun and games, clothes, ideas, holidays, secrets
and confidences. On this day, Anita has a particular
confidence that she wants to share with Lucy. It is up to
you what the subject of the confidence is. You are both
sitting on the grass in your garden, soaking up the sun
on a lovely summer's day, when Anita lets her friend into
her confidence.'

The Political Speaker
'We're going to do a scene that takes place at Speakers'
Corner in Hyde Park. Have you every been there?

Religious and political speakers stand on their soap boxes airing their opinions, and many of them are very colourful personalities. If you haven't yet been to Speakers' Corner it is worth a visit.

'Davidson, you are a political speaker – and a very lively one! I'll leave the choice of subject to you – you may be putting over your view on Northern Ireland, the Arabs and the Israelis, Women's Liberation, the Government, political parties . . . whatever you like. You are interrupted intermittently by hecklers (from the rest of the class). Make sure, hecklers, that you don't get out of control because for the purposes of theatre even if the situation gets a bit wild it must not get chaotic. So, hecklers, work with one another, not against one another. Self-discipline is important, in a crowd scene particularly. All right, Davidson, get on your soap box, and the rest of the class gather round him and listen.'

Miss World

For this piece of work there is a compere and a number of contestants: Miss Australia, Miss Nigeria, Miss Peru, etc. As each contestant's name is called, she walks forward, to the accompaniment of suitable music, and is given a thirty-second interview by the compere about her hobbies, ambitions, what she will do with the prize money if she wins, and so on. Then the result is announced and the winner is crowned while the losers bravely try to hide their disappointment. The situation can be sent up slightly, but without playing for laughs.

The same thing can be done with the sexes reversed, making it a Mr World contest.

Technical dialogue

A type of work that stretches verbal fluency is situation drama in a setting that requires the use of technical dialogue, e.g. a surgical operation, the control cabin of an airliner, a space vehicle. The more authentic vocabulary that can be brought in the better; if it is not authentic, then it must have the right style and sound to it. For science fiction, strings of letters and numbers are useful: 'The LRQs are on. CYP is negative, zero zero zero three. AGS thirty-five degrees. Firing retros. Three. Two. One. Zero.'

Free improvisation given partial information
As young people become more experienced, they will be able to create improvisation given less and less information to work on. You may give them a location, a single statement about a character, an item of costume, a hat, a prop, or any combination of these. Choose a couple of people to use these stimuli to create a piece of drama, without preparation, coming to a definite ending within a rough time-limit of two minutes.

For example: 'This table is in a cafe. Gary, sitting at the the table, is twenty-three and has just come out of the Army. Pauline, coming into the cafe, is wearing this pink hat.' Or 'June is waiting at the bus stop. She is a night-duty telephonist, going home. Shefki is also standing there, wearing this pair of dark glasses.'

A variation of this is *The Park Bench*. Two people, 1 and 2, sit on a park bench. They have a conversation. 1 gets up and goes. 3 comes along and sits down. 2 and 3 have a conversation. 2 gets up and goes. 4 comes along and sits down. 3 and 4 have a conversation, and so on indefinitely. Characterization, whether the characters know each other, and the content of the conversation are all left entirely open.

Real-life events
The re-enactment of real-life situations drawn from

newspaper and television stories can make for interesting
work. As well as providing good dramatic material, it
can lead children to examine their own and other
people's feelings more closely, and increase their sense
of awareness.

If you choose situations based on the children's own
experience at home, school, etc., great care must be
taken not to intrude on anyone's privacy, nor to reopen
any recently healed wounds. Also, remember that fairness demands that all sides of an argument should be
equally well represented.

Carry on the story in drama

Another way of doing situation drama is by telling the
beginning of a story to the class, casting it as you go
along, and then leaving it halfway through for the group
to improvise an ending. You will need to lay out a
simple set, suitable for the story, beforehand.

For example: 'Zanna, would you come and sit on this
chair. I'm going to tell a story, and I want you and a
couple of other people to improvise the ending. Right?'

'It was an unusual case. The girl had been picked up
by the police at two in the morning, wandering the
streets. She couldn't have been more than fourteen. No
money; nothing to identify her. She was wearing an
expensive coat, though. The odd thing was that she
wouldn't say a word to anyone. The ward-sister
[beckoning Rita into the scene] has tried everything,
but she could get no response. The girl had eaten her
breakfast though — as if she was starving. The psychiatrist
at the hospital was Dr Payne [beckoning Elvis Payne to
a table on the other side of the room], maybe he'd be
able to help. She looked such an odd little thing, sitting
there with a blank expression on her face. Probably just
ran away from home, thought the sister, and too scared

to say anything. Dr Payne could be relied upon to put
some fancy explanation on it, though. Better call him
in, anyway . . . .'

And the improvisation takes up the story from there
and it ends in any way they want.

Change in a character

Characters change in reaction to the people they're with.
An example of a piece of work that can be used to
illustrate this:

'You, Catherine, are going away on holiday with the
school. You are sitting in the train with your mum,
Lilian, who has come into the compartment to say
goodbye to you, and we hear your conversation. After
a while, in comes Geraldine, a friend of yours from
school, and the three of you talk together. Then the
whistle blows for the train to go and Mum gets out,
leaving the two girls by themselves; you can end in
whatever way you want. Now, Lilian, you're in a
real state about your daughter, because it's the first
time she's been away from home and you hope she'll be
all right. You hope there will be some nice girls with her.
Catherine wishes her mum wouldn't fuss so, and treat
her like a kid; still, it should be a laugh on holiday with
Geraldine, maybe they'll meet some boys. Geraldine's
mum didn't bring her to the station, she left her to find
her own way. She's brought a packet of fags for the
journey.'

Large groups

Situation drama with large groups is difficult. It demands
awareness and concentration from all the participants.
You need to choose situations where in real life a large
group of people interact together for a common purpose,
without splitting up into smaller groups.

Each of these pieces can be introduced by describing the situation and allocating characters, as required. There is no preparation time; what happens in the improvisation is up to the group.

Examples of group situations:

At School: Reactions to hearing your exam marks. (One of the class, as a teacher, reads out the exam marks for the group, ranging from very low to very high, and gives appropriate comments. The class react, without over-reacting, to hearing their own and each other's marks.)

The English Conversation Class: (Teacher, who must be strong. Pupils come from many different countries and although they don't speak very good English it is their only medium of communication. They are all ages; some are students, others are international businessmen. Some are very serious and conscientious. One or two are more interested in the girls than learning English. One turns up late.)

Television Programme: *The Football Panel 'What's Wrong with the Game?'* (Chairman, who must be very strong. Well-respected international player, near to retirement. Hot-headed young star. Referee. Mad Scottish Football Manager. Self-made millionaire, now chairman of Football Club. Sports journalist. Supporters, old and young, including a couple who have been fined for hooliganism. Ticket tout in dark glasses. Supporter's wife. Old-time footballer who played for five pounds a week.)

Case meeting about a boy who's got into trouble with the police. (Head of Social Team, who acts as chairman. Social Worker. The boy's teacher. Leader of his Youth Club. Educational Psychologist. The boy's parents can be brought in later, and then the boy himself.)

Group Therapy. (Psychiatrist. Members of the group

meet once a week. They are well enough to be out of hospital but have problems: Anxiety. Phobias. Alcoholism. Recovery from drug addiction. Young person not getting on with his or her parents. Husband not getting on with wife or vice versa. Shyness. Depression. The idea of the meeting is to discuss each other's problems and help each other.)

5 MONOLOGUES

Thoughts aloud

'Sarmila, would you sit on the ground in the middle of the floor, with your legs out in front of you. Would Claire find a space and do the same, and Broderick, and Haniff, and Rose. You are all in the bath! Not, I hasten to add, in the same bathroom, but each in your own, private bathroom. Let's see you scrubbing your back . . . and washing yourself all over. Let's hear you singing in the bath!'

'Now, some people get their best ideas while in the bath, you know. I want to hear your thoughts, aloud, in the bath. Maybe you think about your ambitions, or your wildest dreams, or maybe your thoughts are more down to earth — your science homework, what to get for your mum's birthday, what's on telly tonight. Your thoughts could be about school, home, family, boyfriends or girlfriends — whatever. Let's hear some of your thoughts in the bath, aloud, one by one. Sarmila? Action . . . .'

Thoughts aloud can also take place in the doctor's or dentist's waiting room, at the bus stop, or at the back of a classroom.

TV Channels

'I am going to be watching three different programmes on television. Each time I ring the bell that means I've changed channels. First, I might be watching a newscaster, then change to a play (it might be comedy, tragedy, kitchen-sink, or whatever), and then I change channels again: this time it's a pop programme.'

'Mario, will you go into the middle and be three different characters in turn — the choice is yours — changing roles each time I ring the bell and switch channels. Select any incidental props and costume now if you need them. At the sound of the bell you switch characters *immediately*, so keep your wits about you as this requires one hundred per cent concentration and quick thinking.'

A variation of TV channels is *Adverts*, with three TV Commercials as content.

The Mirror

'Everyone sometimes looks at themselves in the mirror, taking a long level look, while critically contemplating their physical appearance — your eyes are a bit piggy, your hair is greasy, your skin's got one or two nasty spots, but you've got quite a nice smile, though, you wish you were slimmer — those hips! Mind you, your legs aren't so bad . . . '

'Kim, take the mirror and honestly criticize yourself, or else you can send it up, exaggerating your beauty! After Kim, let's have John Blundell. Do remember, even if you are sending it up, to still play it for real and not for laughs.'

Half a Duologue, or Talking to an Imaginary Person

In this piece of work the individual taking part talks to an imaginary other person, behaving normally, as if the imaginary person is really there. It's important that they should listen to what the other person is saying, and react to what he does.

For example: 'Johanah Sheikh. Sit in the chair in the middle: I want you to talk to an imaginary teacher — not me, but an imaginary teacher. I'll give you the cue "Johanah Sheikh! Stand up!". And you improvise from there. Watch your eye-level — don't make the teacher twelve feet tall or two feet small. Keep a realistic eye-level so we can believe in the situation. Right! "Johanah Sheikh! Stand up!" '

Other imaginary people to talk to:

Boyfriend or girlfriend, flattering you.
Boyfriend or girlfriend, ending the relationship.
Very depressed person.
Old-age pensioner.
New-born baby (you are its mother).
Crowd (you are a political speaker).
A current pop star (specify who it is).
Foreigner (who speaks very little English).
Someone who's borrowed something from you
    without asking.
Friend who is dying.

6 IMPROVISED PLAYS

About four or five children is a good, manageable size for a group to prepare and perform an improvised play. It gets a bit chaotic if the group is any bigger, unless the children are very experienced, and this leads to disappointment.

At first it is best to appoint a director, who should have a strong personality. Although all the children contribute to the content of the play, the director has the last say, and is responsible for the over-all shape of the play.

Before the children set off to prepare plays, you will

have advised them on how to construct one: the characters must be believable and the play must have a good, strong plot; it must have a beginning, a middle and a good, definite ending; also, stress the importance of having the right length for the story, neither too long nor too short — avoiding 'milking' the situation.

The amount of preparation time needed for improvised plays is usually about ten minutes for Juniors (up to eleven) and about fifteen minutes for Secondary (eleven and over) and older. The more open the brief they have been given, the longer they will need. They can be given a title for the play, or a first line or last line, or a theme. Later on, they can be given more time for thought by appointing directors at the end of a lesson, and giving them a title to work on for next time. Soon they will want to write and direct plays entirely of their own devising.

On average, about seven to ten minutes should be sufficient time to allow for a simple improvised play, including setting up, performance and time for constructive comments and criticisms. As in situation drama, comments can be made by yourself and the rest of the audience, but a nice idea is to choose about four members of the class as a panel of 'experts', specially appointed to comment on the play or plays of the day. Some children like to be given points out of ten, and this can be done by the panel.

In comments, one point to concentrate on at the start is the importance of the action being continuous. If two sets are required, they can be placed side by side, instead of altering the set in the middle of the play. Similarly, all announcements should be made together at the beginning rather than having one of the actors come out of character to announce: 'Scene Two. Next morning. In the shed.'

Direction

When the teacher, or anyone else, is directing a play for improvisation that has already been thought out, it is important to present it to the cast in an orderly way or else they will become confused.

A typical sequence is:

1   Basic idea of the plot, expressed in one or two sentences.
2   Casting. Who the characters are and how they're related.
3   Set. How it will be laid out and what it represents.
4   Description of the action and outline of what the characters will say, dividing it up into sections. Make sure everyone knows their starting points, emphasize the key points in the action and concentrate throughout on what the characters are thinking and feeling.
5   Questions.
6   Suggestions.
7   Changes resulting from suggestions.
8   Run-though of any important or difficult sections.
9   Questions again.
10 Costume and props.
11 Music and lighting (if applicable).

The following play titles are suitable for all ages:

The Letter	The Baby
Good News	The Girl with Green Hair
Get Your Hair Cut	Kidnapped
The Doctor and the Patient	Gangsters
Frou Frou, the Wonder Dog,	Marooned on a Desert Island
or The Dog that can do	The Green Paper Bag
Amazing Tricks	In the Middle of the Night
Crime	A Fairy Tale
The Eavesdropper	Family Matters

The Secret Formula
The Box of Chemicals
The Key
The Door Marked 'Private'
Fire
The Hijacker
In the Aeroplane
The Time Machine
The Secret
Grandad
Beauty and the Beast
The Dream
The Man from the Council
Mother and Son
Father and Son
The Boy (or Girl) Who
    Wouldn't Speak
Old Uncle Bayram
The Thieves
Danger at the Zoo
The American Girl
Robbery with Violence
The Stranger at the Door
The Doctor
The Forbidden Planet
The Bomb That Wasn't
The Birthday Surprise
The Conflict
Robots
Bad News
The Bully at the Bus Stop
Shock
Gunman City
The Visitor who Came to Tea
Rat Poison

In the Year 2000
Planet X
Accident
The Black Box
The Special Dress
Incident at the Bus Stop
The Nagging Mother
The Monster
Ebenezer Scrooge
The Hat
Dial M for Murder
Two Workmen
The Haunted House
Whodunnit?
World War II
The Gipsy Fortune-Teller
The Nightmare
Grandma
Spoilt Children
The Truants
Teacher's Pet
Mother and Daughter
Father and Daughter
I Can Read Your Thoughts
Pauline and the Pop Star
Divorce
The Invisible Man
Baby-Snatcher
Poison Gas
The Man-Eating Plant
Grandad's Will
Please Don't Tease
Round the Flats
The Telephone

Additional play titles particularly suitable for younger children:

The Lost Ring	The Broken Window
Can I Have a Pet?	Three Wishes
What a Surprise	The Lost Kitten
The Wicked Witch	Father Christmas
The Boy (or Girl) with the Funny Nose (or Ears, etc.)	

Additional play titles particularly suitable for older boys and girls:

Happiness	Before and After
Jealousy	The Wig
Pregnancy	The Telegram
Prowess	Cattiness
The Bringer of Bad News	Expulsion from School
Cheating at Cards	At the Office
Hands	Suddenly . . .
No Smoking	Smoking
Have you Had It Yet?	The Protection Racket
The Hippie Commune	The Facts of Life
Behind the Scenes at the Wedding	Blood on a Wednesday
The Prisoners of War	We Rule This School
In the Mental Hospital	Witchcraft
The Return of Al Capone	Suspended from School
Learning to Fly	How to be a Lady
Why I Ran Away from Home	Acting Flash
The Prisoner	The Most Important Thing in Life
In the Heat of the Night	The Death of the President
Love and Money	She Loves Me, She Loves Me Not
The Wrong Number Was Right	Everybody Loves Saturday Night
The Worst Thing in the World	Runaway Lovers

Plays given the last line:

Welcome Home.	Don't talk to her like that.
I don't care.	Now look what you've made

Help! Help! Help!
We can't get out.
No. No. No.
You stupid idiot.
Too late.
Don't cry, love.
You must be out of your
    mind.
Now we'll have to start
    all over again.
I wish we could do this every
    day.
The answer is yes.
The answer is no.
This is the end.
I'll tell Miss on you.

me do.
You've only got yourself
    to blame.
No, it can't be.
We found out too late.
I didn't mean it, honest I
    didn't.
Why me?
It's not my fault.
Please don't tell anyone.
How can I ever thank you
    enough.
Well, thank God for that.
You're fired!
Oh my God he's (or she's)
    dead.

Plays given the first line:

Are you new here?
What's the matter with you?
Ow! The dog is biting my leg.
Sssh! She's coming.
Are you mad?
Where's the baby gone?
Hey mum, look what the
    cat brought in!
Have you got the right
    time?

Hello, what's your name?
Listen, I've got a great idea.
Come here immediately!
My purse is missing!
I wouldn't do that if I were you.
Blimey! look what we've got here.
Turn down that record-player,
    will you?
Your breakfast's getting cold.
I'm feeling fed up.

Themes for plays:

Love.
Plays with titles from current popular song titles.
Plays with proverbs as titles. (All that glitters is not
    gold. Still waters run deep. What the eye doesn't
    see, the heart doesn't grieve over. Two's company,
    three's a crowd.)

A play in which three words drawn from a hat are to
   be used (e.g. Key. Lift. Button. Glass. Sellotape.
   Poster. Vacuum Cleaner. Cake. Heart. Onion. Chalk.
   Cheese. Light. Grass. Bed. Farm. Nails. Angel. Pin.
   Hairbrush. Dandelion. Medicine. Vase. Shoes. Toilet.
   Paper. Wig. Boots. Pig.).
Plays with plots based on current newspaper stories.
Plays which must be set in the future, or which must be
   set in the past.
Plays in which a given prop must be used (e.g. a tankard,
   a pack of cards).
Plays with a supernatural theme.
Topical plays (e.g. Valentine's Day. St. Patrick's Day.
   Hallowe'en. April Fool's Day. Christmas. Guy
   Fawkes.).
Social themes (e.g. A play about a girl who finds herself
   pregnant: her reactions and those of her boy friend,
   other friends, parents, doctor, etc.).
Themes based on work in school outside drama.

SIX

Technique

As we said in the Introduction, regarding the distinction between drama and theatre, in drama an enriched experience is shared by members of the participating group; in theatre, through the use of technique, people not involved in the action can share the experience too. Because of the desire of most children to communicate with others in this way, for them drama develops inevitably towards theatre. Theatre is an art and, as in all art forms, there are skills to be learned — the skills of theatre technique.

Theatre technique should not be treated as an isolated subject but can be brought incidentally and unobtrusively into most classes, as the need for it arises.

If this is not done, children will be held back from realizing their potential. They will have something they want to communicate, but they will be deprived of the most effective way of doing so. Too little will have been asked of them.

To some, performance is a dirty word. It is certainly not beneficial if it is attempted without having the necessary strong foundations in play and drama. If this is done, too much will have been asked of the children rather than too little. Through trying and failing, their confidence may be destroyed, or they may be reduced to the level of parrots, mouthing lines learned by heart for an audience without regard to what they mean. That may be performance of a kind, but nothing worthwhile will be communicated.

Here, then, are a selection of drama ideas that have a strong technical content.

CONCENTRATION

Mind Concentration. This can be done at the start of a
drama session or at any other time when it is necessary
to restore a calm atmosphere. The class form a circle and,
on the teacher's instruction, all close their eyes. The
teacher, in a clear, quiet, deliberate voice, begins 'The
word concentration means "keeping your mind on something" and if you concentrate on what you're doing,
whether it's drama or football or school work, you're
going to do it that much better than if you've got half
your mind on it and the other half on what's on telly
tonight.' Pause while everyone concentrates. 'Now,
listen to all the sounds outside this room.' Pause. 'And
now listen to all the sounds inside the room.' Pause.
'Open your eyes.'
Active Concentration. The circle breaks up and each
person finds a partner. Get them to talk *at each other.*
They must concentrate on two things: one, what they
are saying to their partner; two, what their partner is
saying to them. Every now and then freeze them and test
at random: 'Penny, what was John talking about? John,
what was Penny talking about?' Change partners and
continue this active concentration exercise but this time
they sing at each other, say, 'Doh a Deer' and 'Frere
Jacques' or songs of their own choice. Ask one couple to
sing by themselves; they must not break concentration
by laughing and both must sing their different songs
simultaneously and in full throat.
Clapping Concentration Exercise. Divide the class into
pairs and each pair into A and B. They have to devise
a distinct rhythmical clapping pattern between them.
Then all the A's go to one side of the room and the B's
to the other side, sitting with their backs to each other.
The teacher selects someone from the A side to begin

clapping his rhythm. As soon as his partner from the B side recognizes his clapping pattern he joins in. Repeat several times, starting alternately with side A and side B. *Tongue Twisters* require concentration, as well as being a speech exercise. Start with an easy one, 'furious thrushes', repeated several times. Then progress through 'Peter Piper picked a peck of pickled peppers' and 'She sells sea shells on the sea shore' to 'The sixth sick sheik's sixth sheep's sick' which, according to *The Guinness Book of Records*, is the hardest tongue twister in the English language. If they can manage that at fair speed, then their concentration is very good indeed.

PROJECTION

The aim in projection is not just to speak loudly enough to enable everyone in the room to hear you, but also to speak clearly and distinctly. One person goes to one end of the room and another to the furthermost point opposite. Concentrating on voice projection without in any way straining the voice, they speak in turn to one another. They can be asked to have a conversation with one another on any given subject, or to play Word Tennis (see page 25), which is alternately calling out words from a given category (e.g. meals, flowers, products advertised on television).

The 'carry-on-story' and 'one-word-story' ideas (see page 33) can both be used for voice projection exercises too. If four people are taking part, each can go to a different corner of the room, and each person must be clearly audible to the other three.

METHOD

The title is from the American idea of method acting, i.e. losing yourself completely in the part. In *Method* we are working along similar lines, but in this case by

becoming inanimate objects. For example, you may say
to the class 'Everybody find a space . . . . Be a knife'.
Everyone will get into knife-like positions, with hands
together in the air, or sticking out like the blades of a
penknife, or lying down on the ground, all with knife-like
expressions on their faces. They will, as it were, be
feeling what it is like to be a knife. Encourage them to
use their own idea of a knife, and not to copy each other.
Strike as total credibility.

Other inanimate objects that can be suggested are: a
pair of scissors, the sun, a star, a scarf, a dress on a
hanger, a pencil, a shoe, a bag, a table, a puppet, a banana,
a cake, a ship, a kite, a potato, a flame, a ball, a clock,
a jug, a tree, a box, spectacles, flowers, a bottle, the
numbers 0—9, the letters of the alphabet.

The idea is to foster total belief in what you are doing.
This does not only serve to make for credible perfor-
mances, it is necessary for worthwhile drama of any sort.

This can be done with all ages from infants to adults.
Younger children will take to it very readily.

VOICE MODULATION

Make a sound on a monotone. Get the class to sound a
monotone and explore using different pitches. The voice
modulates when talking — it varies in tone, volume and
pitch. Do the following voice modulation exercises,
bringing home the use of inflexion (e.g. the voice going
up when asking a question), facial expression and
emotion.

Take the sentence 'I can't see you tonight' (or 'Please
don't do that to me', 'What about by brother?', 'I don't
want to go home', or whatever) and ask a small group of
about six people each to take a turn at saying it in
different ways, starting off straight with no particular
expression, then asking a question, answering a question,

being angry, bored, frightened, proud, jeering, surprised, shy, outraged, shouting it as loud as possible (but without straining), whispering (but still projecting), sleepy (while suppressing a yawn), crying (but still the words must be clear), laughing, conspiratorially, in opera style, in pop style.

Take some gibberish, such as 'Gabbitas Motor Thing' or 'Carrie Alley Dot', and ask people individually to use the nonsense words to ask a question and to give the answer. 'Gabbitas Motor Thing? Gabbitas Motor Thing.' The class *listens* and will notice the different modulations in question and answer. The same varied emotions as before can be applied to the gibberish (angry, bored, etc.), but always sincerely. They must really mean it.

INFLEXIONS

Use simple words like 'yes', 'no' and 'oh' to explore the use of varying inflexions, either working individually or as a whole group; e.g. in twos, improvise a piece using only the words 'yes', 'no' and 'oh', letting the inflexions and the actions express the meaning. Or have one person on the telephone holding a conversation with an imaginary person at the other end of the line using only 'yes', 'no' and 'oh' with different inflexions. Inflexions of anger, delight, boredom, fear, surprise, etc. can be brought in. Divide the class into pairs and ask them to talk together using only nonsense words, or numbers, names of colours, or letters of the alphabet and allow the inflexions to express the meaning.

VERBAL MACHINES

Verbal machines are a good follow-up to *Machines* (see page 50). Choose a subject—school, for example—and ask someone to start off a School Machine. He comes out from his place and starts a repetitive verbal pattern

'What page, sir?' . . . 'What page, sir?' . . . 'What page, sir?', making the same movement each time, looking up at the imaginary teacher. He continues doing this without a break, while a second person is beckoned in to build up the next part of the machine, fitting in rhythmically with 'That's *my* pencil' . . . 'That's *my* pencil' . . . 'That's *my* pencil', and then a third chimes in, fitting his phrase in with the other two, 'I can't see the board' . . . 'I can't see the board' . . . 'I can't see the board'. The machine can be stopped by 'Freeze' and started again by 'Action'. Rhythm, timing and projection are three important points of technique here. The different machine parts can be spoken from different levels: standing, sitting, kneeling, or lying down. Three people working together is a good number to make up a verbal machine but more, indeed the whole class, can be used.

Other types of verbal machines include a Teacher Machine, a War Machine, a Food Machine, a Fashion Machine, a TV Machine, a Pop Machine, a Theatre Machi a Hairdresser Machine, a New-born Baby Machine, and many more.

Other categories are verbal machines using different *emotions*: an Angry Machine, a Frightened Machine, a Love Machine, or a Mad Machine; or *Contrasting Machines*: the Insults Machine and the Compliments Machine, the Noisy Machine and the Quiet Machine. A Quiet Machine has a particularly calming effect.

SNEEZE, COUGH, LAUGH, CRY, ETC.

The boys and girls form a circle. Ask them all to start to sneeze, then cough, laugh, cry, yawn, hiccup, belch, stammer in a realistic way. Then, individually, one tells us something about himself, only he punctuates it with sneezing; someone else tells us something about himself punctuating his story with coughing, another laughing, crying, yawning, etc.

It is important to sustain the train of thought by thorough concentration, and of course each person must create for himself a reason for laughing, or crying, or whatever it is.

The most difficult one of sneeze, cough, laugh, cry, etc. to produce is laughing. Work can be done on different kinds of laughter: sniggering, uncontrollable laughter, mocking laughter, sarcastic laughter, laughter at a *risqué* joke, polite laughter, embarrassed laughter, belly-laughter, even laughing yourself to death. This can be done with a whole class, in groups or individually.

ASIDES

Make reference to Shakespeare's use of the aside and the two voice pitches used — the straight one, which the actor uses to the character he is talking to, and the other, lower pitched, out front to the audience or to a third party. Comedian Frankie Howerd is a master of the aside.

For an exercise on asides, two people have a conversation on a given subject, e.g. husband talking to wife about mother-in-law coming to stay. He starts in a straight voice 'So your mother's coming to stay again?' and, in an aside, turning to the audience and dropping his voice a tone 'Interfering old busy-body'. Back to straight voice again: 'Why does she always have to come on a Sunday when I like to have a drink with the boys?' Then to the audience in an aside: 'She does it on purpose, I know, just to make trouble with me and the wife.'

A telephone can be useful in an exercise on asides, the actor talking straight to the person on the phone and, with hand over mouth piece and lowering the voice, making the asides to someone else in the room.

Asides can be done in a genuine way, or else with humorous intent.

STAGE FALLS

Without going far into the technicalities of stage fighting and stunt work, it might be a good idea to try some stage falls, which are popular with children.

In a stage fall the two requirements are to fall realistically but at the same time to avoid hurting yourself.

To avoid hurting yourself a number of things are required. You must fall on parts of the body which are well padded — notably the bottom — and avoid hitting sensitive places such as elbows, knees and head, or jarring your wrists. If possible, break your fall, instead of taking the full force of it in a single impact. You must make sure there are no hard objects, or people, in your way. If you wear spectacles, you should take them off when practising stage falls.

For realism, you must know the reason why you are making the fall as this, of course, will considerably affect the type of fall it is. Has someone shot you with a pistol? Were you knocked down in a brawl? Is it a faint? Have you dropped down dead with a sudden heart attack?

If it is a death fall, then the aftermath is important — concentrating on complete stillness.

When practising stage falls it is necessary to have plenty of room for each person and only three or four people working at the same time to avoid clashing of heads, etc. The signal, representing the gunshot or whatever, is given by the teacher, either to each person individually, or all at once.

Afterwards you can test for relaxation as in 'curl and stretch' (page 42).

EYE CONTACT

The class go into pairs. In an atmosphere of serious concentration, each pair looks into each other's eyes. Continue to hold this mood for fifteen or twenty seconds. Introduce different emotions in turn — hostility, fear, friendliness, boredom — the exercise is to maintain eye contact in that emotion, fearful eyes to fearful eyes, friendly eyes to friendly eyes, etc. The eyes are a most important feature in drama and theatre, as they are such an expressive part of the body. Children can be encouraged not to be afraid or embarrassed when making eye contact, particularly between the sexes. This is important, not only for drama or a theatrical performance, but also when meeting people, in interviews and so on.

STANDING, WALKING AND SITTING

This is an advanced exercise in which everyone in the group takes part together. To work properly it depends on 100 per cent concentration from everybody.

The class sit on chairs in a large circle. The teacher selects a mood or character-state for all the group to adopt. For example, he may say 'You are good-humoured, cheerful people, on good terms with yourselves most of the time, and not easily depressed' and the group become good-humoured people, not by producing any obvious visible signs of good humour in a crude way, such as grinning all over their faces, but by creating the inner feeling of being a good-humoured person. In other words, the emphasis is on being rather than doing.

After allowing a few moments for the feeling to develop, the teacher says someone's name and that person gets up from his place, walks to a vacant chair in the circle, and sits down again, maintaining the same good-humoured mood throughout. Then someone else does the same thing, and someone else again. Keep it up for one to two minutes and then change the mood to something else.

Other moods or character-states that can be used are: self-confident, self-conscious, arrogant, depressed, successful, harassed, undisciplined and frivolous, fit and athletic, intense, relaxed, aggressive, dominant, preoccupied, narcissistic, indecisive.

Exaggeration must be avoided.

VOX POP

Vox populi (voice of the people) is a technique used in current affairs and magazine-type tv programmes, in which a series of interviews on a given subject are conducted with members of the public, and then short sections are edited out of each interview and shown as an uninterrupted sequence.

In a vox pop improvisation, five or six people are asked to stand in a line and produce the same effect as in vox pop on television. For example, you may tell them 'I want you to imagine that you (either being yourself or a different character) have been stopped in the street and interviewed about Crime, the rising crime rate, what should happen to criminals when they're caught, the effect of people's environments on whether they become criminals, and so on. Think about what you might have said. We're going to see just a sentence or two from each interview. Action.' Starting from one end of the line we hear a middle-aged housewife, 'I think it's disgraceful, the way things are going round here; you can't go outside your front door'; straightaway on to the next person, a youngish man, 'Mind you, I don't blame the kids for what they get up to. I'd do the same if I was their age'; another woman, more aggressive, 'I'd soon put a stop to

it, I can tell you. Lock them *all* up, that's what I'd do';
an older man, 'Next thing I knew I woke up in hospital.
Concussion and twenty-five stitches in my head'; an
impassive-faced man, 'I don't know anything about it,
mate'.

This demands quick thinking and concentration, and
also the ability to be economical with words and
condense as much as possible about a character into a
short space of time.

To introduce the technique, simple questions can be
used, like 'What's your favourite meal? What's your
favourite animal and why? What do you look for in a
holiday?' Other topics are politics and current affairs,
television, education and opportunities for young people,
moral questions such as sex before marriage, divorce, etc.

You can pick out one or two characters you find
interesting and ask them more questions about themselves
and the subject. Later on, you can make the exercise even
more testing by having only two people, each one doing
alternate characters, or even only one person doing five
or six characters one after the other.

Vox pop can be used as a lead-in to either discussion
or character work; it is also a useful device for perfor-
mances.

DRAMA VOCABULARY

Just like any other specialized subject, drama has its
own vocabulary and this can be brought in to drama
lessons as the need arises.

The use of simple drama vocabulary not only helps
in expressing things briefly and precisely, but children
respond favourably and it helps to instil an outlook that
is professional, in the sense of being serious-minded and
aiming for high standards. (See over for list of
definitions.)

Improvisation	Making it up as you go along, using your own words.
Mime	Acting with actions but without words.
Props	Properties: the items, other than costumes and scenery, used in drama.
Freeze	Stop absolutely still like a statue.
Action	Begin the action of the drama.
Cut	Stop the action of the drama.
Dialect	Different accents; different ways of speaking English.
Applause	The clapping of an audience.
Encore	A French word meaning 'again', used when asking for a repeat performance.
Audience	The people who watch a performance.
Playwright	Someone who writes plays, e.g. William Shakespeare.
Script	A play, written down.
Dialogue	Conversation in a play.
Corpsing	Laughing when you shouldn't be.
Set	The set represents the place where a scene happens.
Costume	The clothes worn in a play.
Project	Speak loudly and clearly enough to be heard by everyone.
Concentrate	Keep your mind on the job in hand.
Director	The person in charge of a drama event.
Cue	Signal for next performer to being action.
Prompt	Reminder made to an actor if he forgets his words.
Wings	Sides of a stage.
Proscenium	A picture-frame stage.
Theatre-in-the-round	Theatre with the audience on all sides.
Tragedy/Comedy	A tragedy is a sad play, a comedy is a happy one.
Monologues/ duologues	A monologue is one person talking, a duologue is two people talking.
Professional/ amateur	Professional actors are those who are paid to act; it is their job. Amateurs do it for th love of it; as a hobby.